M*oney,*
oney,
oney

CONTRIBUTORS TO

MONEY, MONEY, MONEY

Jacob Needleman

Vicki Robin and Joe Dominguez

Lynne Twist

C. Holland Taylor

Paul Hwoschinsky

Shakti Gawain

Alan Reder

Bernard Lietaer's photo was not available

Quotes about Michael Toms

"...one of the best interviewers who has ever worked the American airwaves, radio, or TV."
— Robert Fuller, physicist, educator, past president of Oberlin College, and chairman of Internews, Inc.

"Someone with whom I have cruised some important realms of the cosmic ocean and in doing so have developed ever-increasing confidence in his intuitive navigation."
— R. Buckminster Fuller (1895–1983), inventor of the geodesic dome; designer, philosopher, and creator of the World Games

"...Bill Moyers and Michael Toms are alike: two of the most creative interviewers it has been my good fortune to work with."
— Joseph Campbell (1904–1987), mythologist and author of *Hero with a Thousand Faces, The Masks of God, Myths to Live By,* and *The Mythic Image*

"In my experience, you are the best interviewer in the world (and having been interviewed in over 35 countries, I speak with authority). Your questions are so deep, showing true inner knowledge and reflective understanding of the issues your interviews are raising, and you provide so warm and yet so focused a set and setting for the interview that you create a context in which we begin to understand what one is really about."
— Jean Houston, Ph.D., author of *A Mythic Life* and *A Passion for the Possible*

"I have always admired Michael's ability to synthesize complicated ideas and get to the heart of the matter. He is creative and imaginative, with an enthusiasm that comes from truly understanding the material and applying it in his own life."
—Charles Garfield, Ph.D., clinical professor at the University of California, San Francisco School of Medicine; author of *Peak Performers;* and co-author of *Wisdom Circles: A Guide to Self-Discovery and Community Building in Small Groups*

✻ ✻ ✻

The Search for Wealth and the Pursuit of Happiness

Jacob Needleman
Joe Dominguez
Lynne Twist
C. Holland Taylor
Paul Hwoschinsky
Shakti Gawain
Vicki Robin
Alan Reder
and
Bernard Lietaer

with Michael Toms

Hay House, Inc.
Carlsbad, CA

Published and distributed in the United States by:
Hay House, Inc., P.O. Box 5100, Carlsbad, CA 92018-5100
(800) 654-5126 • (800) 650-5115 (fax)

Edited by Michael Toms, Rose Holland, and the Hay House editorial staff
Introduction, Prologues, and Epilogues by Michael Toms
Designed by Hay House, Inc.

Library of Congress Cataloging-in-Publication Data

Money, money, money : the search for wealth and the pursuit of happiness / Jacob Needleman . . . [et al.] with Michael Toms.
p. cm.
ISBN 1-56170-458-X (pbk.)
1. Finance, Personal—Moral and ethical aspects. 2. Money—Moral and ethical aspects. 3. Investments—Moral and ethical aspects.
I. Needleman, Jacob. II. Toms, Michael.
HG179.M5967 1998
332.024—dc21 97-30584
CIP

ISBN: 1-56170-458-X

01 00 99 98 4 3 2 1
First Printing, June 1998

Printed in Canada

CONTENTS

APPENDIX

Preface

About New Dimensions

New Dimensions Radio is the major activity of the New Dimensions Foundation, a nonprofit educational organization. "New Dimensions" is an international radio interview series featuring thousands of hours of in-depth dialogues on a wide variety of topics. **Michael Toms,** the co-founder of New Dimensions Radio, the award-winning host of the "New Dimensions" radio interview series—and a widely respected New Paradigm spokesperson and scholar himself—engages in thoughtful, intimate conversations with the leading thinkers and social innovators of our time, focusing on creative and positive approaches to the challenges of a changing society.

About This Book

Money has become a dominant force in human affairs, and it behooves all of us to examine our relationship to money and how it operates in our life. The insights revealed here are meant to guide each of us toward a more conscious use of money. This book brings together several of those who are looking at money and its use in new and different ways, all of which are oriented to creating a better and more equitable world for everyone.

A common thread that unites all of the contributors here is their belief that money and spirit are connected and that each of us has the power to choose the way we will interact with money.

Within these pages, your attitudes and beliefs about money and how the economic system works may be challenged. Keep an open mind, accept what feels right to you, and discard what doesn't. The important point is that all of us can afford to have more clarity about money.

❋ ❋ ❋

Please note: Throughout this book, the interviewer's questions are in italics.

Introduction

The focus of this book is on transforming our attitudes, mindsets, and perception of money so that we can choose how money intersects with our lives and not be a victim of the addictive money system we have created in the West—and are now exporting globally. Each of the contributors to this volume speaks about reclaiming personal power over money and using money in more conscious ways.

For too long, economics and the money system have been defined by economists, politicians, bureaucrats, and bankers whose principal emphasis is on figures, interest rates, percentage of return, and the bottom line; and less on human values and implications. We have need of a holistic vision of money that encompasses ethics, human values, community, and spiritual concerns—one that creates more equity for everyone on the planet and actualizes sustainable use of the world's resources, as well as economic sufficiency for all of the world's inhabitants. This is a tall order and will clearly involve those of us who live in the United States taking a long, hard look at our personal consumption patterns and becoming more clear about wants and basic needs—recognizing that the wheels of commerce and economic growth in this culture currently encourage us at every turn to buy and consume more, not less. Being willing to examine our personal relationship to money is at the core of any creative shift in how the planet interacts with it.

Within these pages, you will find a wealth of insights about how we can increase our awareness of money and begin to become more conscious about how we use it. Philosophy professor **Jacob Needleman** gets us started by making the connection between money and meaning and points to the spiritual side of money. The late **Joe Dominguez** suggested that we can escape the "money trap," giving us ways to go about doing that. He is followed by fund-raiser extraordinaire **Lynne Twist**, who speaks about how money and soul are related through how we allocate our financial resources. **C. Holland Taylor** addresses the economic institutions and policies that need to be transformed. Former venture capitalist **Paul Hwoschinsky** redefines wealth by showing us that true wealth is much more than how much money we have.

Personal growth pioneer **Shakti Gawain** speaks about what real prosperity encompasses and how we can create it in our own lives. Again, **Joe Dominguez** returns with his partner, **Vicki Robin**, to explain how we can create financial independence and have a choice about whether we want to continue making more money. Author **Alan Reder** tells us about the relevance of socially responsible investing and how we can use our money to catalyze constructive social change. Last but not least, engineer, currency trader, former investment fund manager, and university professor **Bernard Lietaer** paints a vision of the future of money and economics that excites the imagination and inspires the mind and heart.

This book opens the door to a whole new world of money, wealth, and meaning. It is up to each of us to walk through the doorway.

— Michael Toms
Ukiah, California
March 1998

⁂

CHAPTER ONE

Money and the Meaning of Life

Jacob Needleman and Michael Toms

PROLOGUE

Money is a compelling force in our society. We make it, spend it, save it, lose it, bet it, dream about it, and worry about it. Money impacts our lives in many ways. On a global scale, money and economic forces shape national agendas; create conflict and wars; and produce social unrest, injustice, and oppression. Money finds its way into literally every aspect of life on the planet. So it behooves us to understand money more fully and see how it impacts and relates to the meaning of our lives. This is our focus with Jacob Needleman, professor of philosophy at San Francisco State University, and the author of many books, including Lost Christianity, The New Religions, The Way of a Physician, Time and the Soul, *and* Money and the Meaning of Life. *Here, we are going to explore money and the meaning of life with Jacob Needleman.*

❋ ❋ ❋

MICHAEL TOMS: *As a philosopher, what first got you interested in money?*

JACOB NEEDLEMAN: Throughout my life and career, I have tried to relate the great ideas of spiritual and ancient traditions and the great questions of philosophy that have been asked for thousands of years to contemporary problems that we actually experience in our day-to-day lives. The questions of meaning and purpose and the nature of reality are eternal questions. We may not always find answers in the way that we are used to finding answers, but attempting to answer those questions is part of what it means to be human. And the more deeply those questions can be explored, the more human we can become.

In our daily lives, there are also problems to be solved, things to be fixed, and needs to be taken care of. I've been searching to find the relationship between the great philosophical questions and contemporary problems. I wanted to see if these ancient teachings could really throw a useful light of understanding on the problems that we experience and on the lives that we lead in our culture. I have worked with questions in education, science, medicine, psychology, and religion. And for years it's been very clear—although I didn't know how to approach it—that the one problem, the one force, the one factor that all of us must face, sometimes suffer from, and often seem unable to deal with is the money question.

For years, I've wondered how one can look at money from the perspective of the great teachings. It seems so hard to find a place for the money question within that framework without idealizing it and sentimentalizing it into something unrealistic. On the other hand, it is hard not to be swallowed by it and have it cut off entirely from our inner quest. In a way, this subject has been at the back of my mind for years and years. I've never known exactly how to approach it. I just knew it had to be faced in some way. To my mind, if spiritual ideas don't throw light on how we actually live, then they are of limited use.

In terms of spiritual traditions and religion and their relationship to money, how does Western culture relate to money differently from cultures in the Middle East and Asia? Have Westerners been impacted by money in the way someone in Asia has been impacted by money?

In our culture, particularly in America, money has entered into more aspects of human life, in my opinion, than it has ever entered in to in any culture before. It's not that human beings haven't always been greedy or materialistic in some sense, but the money itself—as a device, an instrument, a reality—enters in to every aspect of life now. You can't do a thing without, in some way, facing the money question. How people react to this modern development of money varies from culture to culture, from epoch to epoch. A Russian responds differently to money than an American. Money means different things to different people. In a way, it's one of the keys of self-knowledge to see how individuals behave in relation to money. There are cultures in which honor is the main thing—self-respect and honor. There are other cultures in which beauty or power is the main thing. But for our culture, very often money occupies the central purpose of life. It is the thing that everybody wants. It is not the thing everybody wants in Russia or in Iraq. No matter how much they may fight for it or look for it, it is not their ultimate goal. When you penetrate beneath the surface, something else is very often there. But in our society, the one thing that brings us all together is that we all want money.

Money is so often seen as the means to other ends, but with the knowledge that we can't have the other ends without the money.

If we were really to use money as a means to an end, it would be relatively more healthy. In reality, money has become an end. If you ask people, they'll say, "Yes, maybe it's a means to an end." But, in fact, how people behave indicates that money is an end in itself. So the *instrument* has become the *end*—which is one of the pathologies of our relationship to money.

One of the interesting aspects of the Persian Gulf war is that one watched the news reports on television and heard them on the radio. So often the news reports would be punctuated with "the Dow Jones went up or down today." And it was almost a direct correlation to what was happening in the war. In other words, there was this connection with the economic reality of the United States and this other reality that was taking place on the sands of Arabia.

This points again to the idea that money represents a huge force in human life. It may be why more and more there is war. Money may be connected to other things. It may be connected to art, science, the pursuit of knowledge, and the pursuit of spiritual development. One of the questions in my book *Money and the Meaning of Life* is: If your search is for inner development, what is a normal, beneficent, or regenerative relationship to the force of money? That question, in written form, I have not seen treated by anyone. And there is a good reason for that. It's extremely hard to think intelligently about it. Do you know anyone who is really normal with money? Whenever I ask that question, I find that we don't even know what it means to be normal with money. I think that money has become, for our generation, what sex was for earlier generations: a force that is behind almost everything people do. This is an idea that we are not yet able to face without hypocrisy. It's almost as if there is as much of an inability to face the money question today as there was an inability to face the sexual question 50 years ago. There's more hypocrisy about money than about almost anything. These days, if you ask people about their sexual habits, in two or three minutes you will get more information than you want. But ask people how much money they make! Money is very volatile, very alive. If the quest for self-knowledge means to know yourself as you really are, then you are going to have to study how you are in relation to money.

What is the association that we make between money and evil? Money and sin?

It's difficult in terms of the history of Western tradition and Christianity to sort it all out. It's a complex issue, but there are some very simple points. Major religions of the world, such as Judaism, Islam, and Christianity, speak against usury. There were many laws against usury, but today, we have a culture that is founded on credit.

In other cultures, other times, when you went to borrow money, it was only because you really needed it. It was considered a sin to take advantage of someone in desperate straits. That was the spiritual reason, the humane reason against usury. But when you have a country, an economy, that is based on credit, then of course previous ideas become meaningless, and the concept has to be restated.

"Money is dirty. Sex is dirty." Why are these things considered dirty, particularly in Western, puritanical culture? What's the real reason, and what's the hypocrisy there? Of course we know that the love of money is the root of all evil. Well, it's not money that is the root of all evil; it's the *love* of money. Now, the love of money means attachment to it. It's a form of the sin of idolatry. And what is idolatry? It means trying to get ultimate meaning out of that which cannot provide ultimate meaning. Ultimate meaning can only come from God, from the spiritual force in ourselves. So the sin of money and loving money lies in trying to get from that which is not the highest, only what the highest can give. It's an illusion to have that view about money. In my mind, that is the origin of the sin of money, as well as sex. None of these things were originally in the great teachings of Christianity, Judaism, Islam, Hinduism, or Taoism. None of these religions ever considered it evil to desire what money can buy, to desire sexual satisfaction, or to desire food.

What is evil is when you give more to money than you need to, and try to get out of it what it cannot bring you. In that sense, I think, people have been trying to get from money what money can't give. Therefore, they sometimes turn away from money as though *it* were the problem. And it's not! The problem is the attachment. The same hypocrisy arises in our attitudes toward money as it does with sex. If love of money is bad, then I won't love money, I'll hate money. If love of sex is bad, I'll hate sex. All that produces is hypocrisy, suppression, and more evil than the original thing would have produced. So the challenge becomes learning how to like money for what money can give, and for no more or less.

We attribute to people with money a certain power and superior qualities that they may not have at all. But because they have money, we relate differently. Where does that come from?

First, we have to recognize, and again, not be hypocritical about, how much we are influenced by the fact that someone has money. During the course of writing the book *Money and the Meaning of Life*, I met a lot of very wealthy people. I found myself feeling that way. I met someone who has a billion dollars, and suddenly I had a different feeling toward him. I had a different relationship with him. I couldn't help it. Unfortunately, I can't say, "Well, I'm free of that."

I also spoke with a person who at 50 years old is one of the richest men in America. He made the money himself. Most people who are very wealthy have either inherited money or done something more or less criminal to get it. It is rare to find somebody who is very wealthy and has made it himself without doing something criminal. Anyway, I asked this man what he felt was the most surprising thing about being rich. He said, "People respect my opinion. I'm invited to be on the board of directors of universities and on government boards. And what do I know? I don't know anything; I'm just rich."

Before one asks *why* such feelings occur, one has to face the fact that they *do* occur. When you acknowledge that these feelings exist, you begin to understand the illusions that foster this attitude. To many people who have money, the way others relate to them is a source of great unhappiness, although sometimes they don't realize what's causing their unhappiness. People relate to them in ways that don't correspond to who they really are—just because they have money. We have this illusion that money brings a kind of power, a kind of competence, a kind of capacity—an illusion that I think we have to penetrate.

At the same time, there is the opposite illusion that having money doesn't mean anything. We also have to realize that someone who makes a lot of money is not necessarily selfish, greedy, or stupid. There are very intelligent people who make money. It takes a certain talent to make a lot of money and to make it without being crooked or criminal about it. Money is the kind of medium through which real things do happen sometimes. Somebody who can work in such a way as to actually make money is someone with a kind of competence. The issue is very complex.

The secret, in my opinion, is to keep it all together and not try to come to simplistic conclusions. We know that money actually makes things happen in the world. How do we deal with that? We know that a relationship between people alters when money enters the picture. For example, you can be very happy with somebody. You can have an intimate relationship. You can feel you love each other. You're kind to each other. You see eye to eye. You help each other. Then, one of you asks the other for a $400 or $500 loan. Immediately, something is revealed that was not there before. One needs to study that revelation and face it sincerely. Or when someone dies in a family and there's an inheritance, watch what happens. It's a minefield that blows up legs, arms, relationships, all sorts of things. It wouldn't be quite such a minefield if people were willing to sincerely face the emotions that are involved with money. I can't answer the question "Why?" But the question has to be asked. It must be open.

I remember someone telling me once that if you want to understand money and how you interact with money, understand who first taught you about money. Go back to where you learned about money, from your mother and father. And there you will discover a lot of wisdom.

It is necessary to see what we learned about money when we were very young. For many of us, money factors were the deepest gut-level emotions that took place in our family life; therefore, if we are going to become different people, more moral people, we cannot do it unless we confront the money question in our lives. Whatever morality we may adopt, it won't stand up to the force of money because those forces were instilled in us when we were very young. They are part of our visceral makeup. So we all have to feel something creatively, risk something with the question of money, when searching for ourselves.

The Depression impacted not only the people who lived at the time it occurred, which was in the 1930s, but it has impacted every generation since then up to the present day. The present leadership generation essentially came out of the Depression, having grown up as children during the Depression. There's almost a survival mentality, as if we've got to get as much as we can get of it because we may lose it at some point. How has that colored decision making and values and ideas? Will we ever get away from the Depression mentality?

I was brought up in a Depression household, so I understand the Depression mentality. It is a viewpoint that sees a kind of brutal, Darwinian world out there, out to screw us, take things away from us. That is certainly a great nightmare vision of how reality functions. We all can observe it. Try sitting down at a bar sometime; half the stories you hear are going to be about "that son of a bitch" and "what he did to me." There's just enough truth in that view of the world that we can't throw it away, but we don't want to be devoured by that nightmare. And to some extent, I think we can get away from that view through sincerity and self-knowledge.

One doesn't want to go to the other extreme, however, imagining a daydream world where everything is nice, where people are anxious to help each other, where everybody is going to give you money, and where you are going to be successful. I don't think a daydream is any better than a nightmare. We have to know just what the realities of a money-driven society are and how they correspond to human desire and human fear. So that we don't go from the depression of what I would call the East Coast nightmare into the fantasy of the New Age daydream, we have to know how to look at things squarely for what they are and realize that it is a tough world. There is such a thing as greed, ego, criminality, and self-deception. But there is also goodness, love, and the need for sustaining relationships. Don't make the decision too quickly about what is true, but try to explore the issue from all angles.

Don't be too afraid of the money question. And don't be too dreamy about it.

Did you find that any of the great traditions have particular relevance to or knowledge or wisdom about money?

One of the things that I say in my book *Money and the Meaning of Life*, which I think might be of interest, is that originally money was a sacred invention. It was created by men and women of considerable vision to allow for a community of exchange and to satisfy the need for economic goods. At the same time, it allowed people to realize their dependence on each other and on God. It was a way to help people be *in* the world effectively without being *of* the world. It addressed what I call the dual nature of humans: the inward divinity and the outward need to survive. In that sense, when you look at the origin of money and how it was ministered by the priests in truly religious societies, you begin to see that yes, there's a great deal of wisdom there.

When it comes to the modern concept of money, however, we can see the changes that have taken place. Money is no longer something as tangible as metal coins. It's no longer even paper—and that represented an enormous change when money became paper. Now, money is synonymous with credit. It's not even credit cards. It's electronic impulses. And the wisdom that was once so much a part of the concept of money and its related problems is now lacking. You don't find anything in religious texts such as the Talmud about credit card debt or that sort of thing, which is a very contemporary problem. But you do find some interesting ideas about material possessions that can be applicable. For example, Maimonides, the greatest of all the Judaic philosophers, mystics, and theologians, says some extraordinarily interesting things in *A Guide for the Perplexed*. Basically, he says that all human ills come from wanting what we do not need—which serves to focus on the fact that there is a difference between needs and desires. It raises the questions: What do we really need, and what do we merely want? Looking at our modern concept of money from that angle, we begin to realize that our economy is based not on the *satisfaction* of desire, but on the *creation* of desire. Desire that is created and then satisfied is a totally unnatural state of affairs.

This economy is based on the creation of ever-new desires, which are then satisfied but not for long. For the economy to flourish, it must perpetuate desire. It must continually create more things for us to want, more things for us to desire, things that we don't really need but that we like. There is a passage in John Kenneth Galbraith's *Affluent Society* that describes how this kind of desire-producing economy works, and with only one or two minor changes in words, it could be an exact description of the Buddhist condition of Samsara that you find in all the Buddhist texts. Samsara is the condition of constantly trying to satisfy cravings that are themselves not natural or authentic. To see an economist describe our culture in such a way that it matches exactly the Buddhist concept of Samsara—that the more you satisfy the desire, the more you want, and that there is no true fulfillment—was a revelation to me.

It seems to me, from my observation, that the Buddhists, the Tibetans, have a particular ability, as I've seen them in this country, to cope with money. They don't seem to talk about it at all, but they seem to be able to manifest it. To what do you ascribe that talent?

Somebody once said that they are really the lost tribe of Israel. When they get more and more into earning money, then we'll see how they handle it. Right now, it's too soon to say. I think they are, thank goodness, the recipients of a lot of generosity and good feeling from the rest of us, and so they are receiving help, but we'll see. It takes time. When they actually have money, we'll have to see how they manage it. One of the problems of any spiritual organization, or person, is that once you've finally gotten money, what does it do to your life? What does it do to your quality of life? The church has had to face that for a thousand years.

Another thing I've noticed over the last 15 or 20 years, and you've probably noticed it yourself, is that when you are dealing with things of the spirit, dealing with things of the soul, and charging money for it, it has a particularly large potential for upset. For example, a major corporation can go along despoiling the environment for 50 years, and nobody says anything. Then, somebody comes along and charges $300 for a workshop that seems to help people (I mean, people come out and say: "I was transformed," or "I received some value from it"). But because there is money involved somehow for this exchange of services or value, there is something wrong about that.

What I say in my book *Money and the Meaning of Life* is that money has entered so much into human life now that if you ask, "What is it that money can buy and what can't it buy?" you're asking a major philosophical, spiritual question. I answer it somewhat cryptically by saying that money can buy everything except meaning. And there are things that money can't buy that come from God, that come from the spirit. Money can't bring you meaning, but it can bring you a lot of other things that are necessary to you. And one of them is the ability to give the workshop, to rent the space, to have the facilities, to survive, to eat.

While I think it is true that there are things upon which you can put no price, things of a spiritual nature, I also think that there is a huge amount of confusion and hypocrisy about matters of the spirit. People living in the world who deal with spiritual matters are somehow thought of as wispy, pure creatures who don't need to rent the hall and pay the bills. This is one of the illusions, that somehow Jesus or Buddha didn't have to eat or pay caravan fare or pay rent for living space. And if you begin to look at the life of Jesus, as much as we can tell about it, or at the lives of any of the great spiritual masters, you will find they had interesting relationships with money. People who were wealthy and helped them were very special to them.

Of course, we see a lot of hypocrisy on the other side as well. There are people who pretend to be spiritual but who are actually making tons of money and conning the public. Just because such people exist, however, doesn't mean that if others have a real spiritual message they should work for nothing. That's ridiculous. It's part of the same hypocrisy that surrounded sexual ideas, too. Somehow a spiritual person shouldn't have a sexual life. That's ridiculous. To assert that spiritual people don't eat food or don't need money is equally ridiculous. But it's an idea that persists. Of course, if you see a guy in spiritual robes driving 29 Rolls Royces, you have every reason to think something funny is going on.

But a real spiritual master, now, and probably in all times, would work with people's relationship to money. If you are going to show people themselves, which is one of the aims of a spiritual master, you have to work with them and their relationship with money. For the spiritual teacher to be able to do that, he or she must be free of the money hang-up, and that's very rare. A lot of gurus are not free of it. Maybe they deceive themselves. Because they are getting all the money given to them, they think somehow they are free of it. But I've seen more than one guru fall. Of course, as we know, during the sixties when the commune experiments were being tried, one of the main things that destroyed them was their lack of a real understanding of the money question.

Often, the leader overestimated his freedom from the money question and overestimated his own freedom. He wasn't that free. So when the leader got money, he became kind of crazy sometimes. Money, sex, and power were the three challenges to the leadership of these communes. As I've said in my book, if you want to know about the measure of a person, one of the main things to look at is how that person behaves with money. It doesn't mean that they deprive themselves of money, but there must be a spiritually creative use of money. That is part of our challenge.

This was touched on earlier, but why is money such a secret? Why is it such a taboo subject? Probably the most intimate question you could ask someone is, "Well, how much did you make last year?"

Somehow, for many of us, again maybe more for men than women, our sense of self-esteem and self-worth and who we are is bound up with our money situation. It is the most private thing in our lives. What is this self-esteem and self-worth and self-identity that's concerned with money? We have to explore that, too.

We also become dependent on money. When I was giving a sociology class the other day, I overheard these young students talking about their credit card problems, and they were all saying, "I can't bear it. These credit cards come, and they are given to me as a young student. It makes me feel grown up. It makes me feel important. Makes me feel I've made it. And here I am stuck at the bottom of a pile of debt, and I don't know how I'm ever going to get out."

In many ways, money can be an addictive substance. One of the people I write about in my book is a man who inherited enormous amounts of money suddenly. I couldn't figure out what it was about him that struck me as familiar. The way he looked. A certain weakness and a certain niceness. Then, I realized this man was like an alcoholic. Only his drug was money. And having suddenly inherited over $60 million, he no longer could face life squarely. Money took the edge off, and money was his way of putting a buffer between himself and the realities of himself, his relationships, and his life. The parallel with alcohol was startling.

I think, in our culture, we're all more or less addicted to the money problem, one way or another. I think that the earning of money, the making of money, is a force now, and nobody—or very few people—really stops to consider how much money is enough. I asked more than one successful business executive. There was one in New York at a big investment firm, and he was a top person there. He was telling me about the billion-dollar deals. And he was a decent person. This was not some caricature. He was even interested in spiritual things. I asked him how much money he thought was enough, and his mouth dropped open. He said, "You know, I never thought of that. I never considered it. Just making money is an end in itself." I think a question that a lot of people should think about is: How much is enough for my life or for any given purpose? There are not many people thinking like that.

The reason it's difficult and so very important is because it's like asking, "What exactly do you want in your life? How much is it going to take to get it?" And most of us don't know what we really want, and the money problem partly expresses that. We seem to say, "Until I find out what I want, I'll just go and make a lot of money. Then, when I finally find out what I want, I'll have enough." But we don't find out what we want, so all we've got is our money, our instrument.

There's not much evidence of alternative routes to follow either. When you look around, most people are doing the same thing. There are no role models out there to really see. You have to look. You have to begin searching around, because the culture only supports you following the traditional route.

We need to be able to find other human beings with whom we can begin to relate on the basis of the search for truth, not just the quest for money. That, to me, is the only hope we have in our culture. And we are free in this culture to be able to associate with whomever we want. To my mind, the beginning of the answer to almost every question in our society lies in establishing a relationship with others who are searching for truth. What does it mean to have a philosophical friend—a friend, a companion, on the way to Truth? With money, as with everything else, we can begin to relate to each other on the basis of sincerity and questioning what we want.

*I think the very word says it. Philosophy—*philos *and* sophos *in the Greek, meaning a "friend of wisdom." The late David Bohm, a physicist, was a person very interested in the origin of words. He explored this whole process of how we communicate and how we interact with one another.*

There are some words that are like a whole philosophy in one word—where it comes from, and the power of a word. There were some languages that were sacred—languages where the *sound* of the word communicated something very strong. I think you could take almost any word, and if you follow it back far enough, what's behind it will surprise you. Also, how people use words is very interesting. For example, I was once at a conference about spirituality, contemplation, and action, and we were all speaking English, of course. We were from different cultures, different countries. There was a man from Nigeria who spoke perfect Oxford English, and he was giving a lecture about the Yoruba religion in Nigeria. He would speak in this very clipped accent, and whenever he mentioned a word from that language—for example, the word *ephay,* he would pronounce it forcefully, using his solar plexus or his belly. Then, he'd go back into his head and continue in the Oxford language.

This was language that not only had different linguistic meanings, its sounds were made using different parts of the human anatomy.

To speak from the heart is not just a figure of speech. There is the voice and where the voice comes from and what the voice communicates. What is a conscious voice? And what is merely a voice that's coming from the head? All of this is part of the very exciting time we're living in. And to get back to our subject, money flows through it all. Money just snakes through everything. So the thesis of my book is really this: Spiritual development is basically an attempt to balance two opposing forces in human nature. We are two-natured beings. One in us moves toward God, and the other moves out toward the world. This is humanity's uniqueness, its glory, and its challenge. To find the force within ourselves that can balance and find the proper place between these two natures is, to my mind, real inner development.

In our time, the outward-directed aspect of human nature is flowing mainly through money; therefore, in order to balance these two natures, first we have to see them for what they are, which means that we have to study ourselves as we are in the midst of money questions. That's where money takes a place in the search for meaning. It's only by really understanding how we are with money that we begin to understand this side of our human nature. I don't know if that's been looked at from that point of view in any book that I've seen. I don't see any other philosopher or spiritual writer exploring this. Many of them write about money, but they do it in such a way that it is tiresome. It's like when people write about sex and say don't give it too much weight and be free. People write about money, and they write religious platitudes such as, "Well, don't be too involved with it, and do things free, and do things for nothing. Don't be greedy." That's not going to work now. We have to see much more honestly how we are with it.

When the check comes at lunch and we see the dance of hypocrisy that goes around the table, we have to see it for what it is and be able to face that we, too, are sort of waiting for the other guy to pick up the check. Even handling money should be examined. When I was a little kid in the Depression, a nickel was a power thing, a dime was mysterious and small, a quarter was magical, and a half-dollar would blow your mind. So one day when I was in third grade, there was the war-bond drive, and I had this very stingy, horrible uncle who never gave anybody anything. Because the war bond was a good investment, he decided he would buy a $1,000 war bond. I was given the privilege of carrying a $1,000 bill, which used to exist in those days, to school, holding it in my hand, while my uncle and my mother walked ten feet behind me to make sure nothing happened to me. But I had a fluctuating sense of the object I held in my hand—it was a $1,000 bill, and at the same time, just a hunk of paper. We've got to see this thing and what it does to us.

I think of going back in history and looking at the gold rush here in California—what gold did to people and still does to people. The phenomenal fascination of gold.

For anybody who wants to understand human beings and human situations and themselves, it really is important to hold some gold in your hands—even if it's just Krugerrands or Maple Leafs. Get a bunch of them, even if you have to buy them for a day. If I were educating people, one of the things I would advise is to go out and just handle gold. Feel it. Begin to understand the power it has had as a symbol. There is a certain magic to it. These are the kinds of things we have to acknowledge. Nobody is free from these things. If most of the human race is greedy and driven mad by gold, for example, I can be pretty sure that I'll be driven mad by it, too, if I face it. When you handle gold, you see all the power it has. You realize that there are many people who would kill for it. Handling gold gives you a feeling of what this force, this outward force of human life, really is. Money is a great thing for that.

Money can be a hard teacher, but it's a very good teacher. It's a great test of your sincerity. It tests your ability to sincerely accept how you are. To me, that's the main teaching method of money. If you really want honest awareness about yourself, try to find conditions in which you can see how you are with money. It means sometimes taking some risks with money. In one of the seminars on money that I gave once, we had an experiment where five people were given a dollar bill or two dollars and told to go out in the street and give it away to the first person they wanted to give it to, but not to somebody begging. It was astonishing—the power of trying to do that and how difficult it was.

❋ ❋ ❋

EPILOGUE

Probing beneath the surface of the cultural illusions about money can begin to bring a more enlightened view of the economic reality, which has become such a dominant force in all our lives. It's not so much seeking ultimate answers, but rather asking new questions about our relationship to money that can begin to dispel the darkness around money. Professor Needleman also emphasizes the relevance of creating relationships and community around money issues. He points out the connection between the search for truth and money and how we mostly avoid seeing the true picture.

We live in a society rampant with money addiction. Money has become an end in itself—money market funds are a prime example of this principle at work. The challenge is to reestablish a moral ethic and return human values to our relationship with money. As we are able to do this in our own lives, we will become more conscious and aware, and in the process, lessen the hold that money has on us in contemporary society.

❋ ❋ ❋ ❋ ❋ ❋

CHAPTER TWO

Money Wisdom

Joe Dominguez and Michael Toms

PROLOGUE

Money is a necessary ingredient in these times. It permeates all of life—personal, social, political, even spiritual life. And yet money and its uses may be the least understood dynamic of our lives. We know we can't do without it. We usually feel we need more of it. And many of us are affected negatively because we have less of it. In a sense, money is the fuel that feeds the engine we have to use, but we don't understand how any of it works. When there are problems, we are in trouble.

In the following dialogue, the late Joe Dominguez (1938–1997) attempted to clear away some of the fog surrounding money so that it becomes less a driving force in our lives and more a tool that we can use to serve us. Joe Dominguez retired at the age of 30 in 1969, not through risky investments, but through working for ten years on Wall Street as a highly respected financial analyst and author of an internationally distributed weekly market letter. Since then, he dedicated all of his time and skill to humanitarian service. He took no money for anything he did. For many years, he presented his seminar, "Transforming Your Relationship with Money and Achieving Financial Independence," internationally. In 1986, Joe donated all rights to produce and distribute his increasingly popular seminar as an audiocassette workbook course to the New Road Map Foundation so that more people could benefit from the program. He co-authored Your Money or Your Life *with Vicki Robin.*

❋ ❋ ❋

MICHAEL TOMS*: When did you first start thinking about financial independence for yourself? When did that first occur?*

JOE DOMINGUEZ: I started thinking about financial independence very early in my life. I grew up in pretty good poverty straits in New York City, and one of the first things I saw was that money seemed to be a source of tremendous confusion for people. As I went through my teenage years and got out of the ghetto, I realized it wasn't just people in the poverty class who were confused about money. I realized that we are somehow conditioned to think that money is going to bring us happiness, but that people who have money aren't any happier. What I concluded was that I needed to learn more about money. And as my own development progressed, I realized that I wanted to learn what money was and learn how to control it so that I wouldn't have to be concerned about it. I knew there had to be more to life than just making a living.

With that in mind, I went to college, got educated as an engineer, and decided to apply that to Wall Street. That was the best place for me to learn about money. I got a job on Wall Street and worked my way up through the ranks for the next ten years. I achieved financial independence by the time I was 30. Then, I began the next phase of my education.

I had to answer the question: What is life really about? I knew that it was not about making money. After a year and a half of a lot of introspection and working with a number of different tools, I came to the conclusion that, for me, life was about serving. I was here to serve the planet.

To achieve that aim, I went through a number of different organizations and projects that I felt were contributing to the welfare of the planet. Then, several years ago, I co-founded the New Road Map Foundation. The foundation was set up to support other organizations that were involved in social change or personal and planetary transformation.

Is that when you started doing the seminar on achieving financial independence?

The history of the seminar is interesting. It began with my telling friends how I'd achieved financial independence. In the years on Wall Street, I had to get very methodical about how I applied what I was learning to my own life. By the time I got out, the process was a complete package for me, but I always thought it was purely personal. I assumed other people would go through whatever processes they needed to go through. But people would ask me how I'd become financially independent at the age of 30. I would share it, and they would be wide-eyed with interest and want to hear more. So, I'd outline the entire process that I used, and they would try it, and it would work for them, too.

As more and more people began to ask about it, it became a seminar. First, there were small groups of 20 to 30 people. As people began to achieve financial independence and see that the plan was feasible, they told their friends about it. Finally, as word continued to spread, the seminars grew to 400 people. And then invitations to do the seminar came in from all around the world. I realized that in order to fill the demand, I would have to clone myself. At the same time, I reminded myself that I had not intended my life to be about giving seminars.

Realizing there were more effective ways to disseminate information than for me to stand on a stage and yell for eight hours, we decided to tape the seminars. And that's how the course came about. We put together the best of the seminars on tape and created a workbook to duplicate what I usually did on a chalkboard. Much to my amazement and pleasure, I found that the tapes and workbook were far more effective. People would write to say how much better the course was than the seminar—and I didn't take that as an insult. It's much more interactive to listen to tapes at your own pace and work things out in a workbook than just to sit and listen to an eight-hour lecture.

There are lots of seminars and workshops and even tapes about money—how to make more of it, how to make it work, how to use it more wisely, how not to be manipulated by it, and so forth. How would you differentiate the work you've done with money versus all those other seminars and workshops and tapes?

One difference is that the other folks—or the ones who I know about—take money for what they do, so they have a vested interest. If they know so much about money, why do they still have to work for it? I don't take any money for what I do. I do charge for the course, but all that money is donated to nonprofit organizations. I don't have to take any money for myself because I am already financially independent. I think that is an important factor, and people have repeatedly told me that it makes what I'm offering much more credible than some theories. Obviously, I've lived it, and I am living it.

Another factor that most other seminars don't deal with is the integration of the whole person with his or her financial life. I sometimes think that people compartmentalize themselves, saying "Here's my everyday life, and here's my financial life." It doesn't work that way. It is an integrated whole. In my course, I deal with many factors, including attitudes, belief systems, and misconceptions about money. Times have changed, yet we still use the same money/work paradigm that was instituted around the time of the Industrial Revolution. So, we have to create a new road map. Triple-A constantly updates its maps, but who updates our maps on something as important as our interaction with money? I discuss these issues in the course, and then I go beyond the psychological, emotional, and spiritual aspects to give the step-by-step process that I developed. These are very pragmatic steps that I took to get entirely out of the nine-to-five workforce.

Most of us think that if we learn how to balance our checkbook and figure out the stock market, we know about money. But we don't ordinarily hear money associated with—as you are suggesting—other parts of our lives. Why is that? What are some of the reasons?

To understand why we think about money in the ways that we do, I think we have to ask ourselves where we got our education about money. Was it from people who were coming from an enlightened understanding of money? Or was it from the economics teacher who was struggling to make ends meet? Or was it from our parents who were struggling just to support us and put us through school? Probably most of our teachers have not been what we could call enlightened teachers. So they perpetrate the myths. I think that is a very important aspect of our beliefs.

One of the things I do in the course is have people define money. Over the years, I've collected remarkably similar answers. The responses are all automatic. Generally, people indicate that money is a means to an end or that money is a source. Very few people know what money is in their own lives, yet they deal with it day in and day out. Creating a personal definition of money—not something out of an economics textbook—is vital. But very few people do that.

What is your personal definition of money?

Money is something for which I have exchanged my life energy. I think it's rather universal to do so—even if the money is inherited. A lot of people who inherit money have to work through a lot of guilt and soul-searching to be comfortable with their situation, and they have to spend time in the lawyer's office signing papers. One way or another, we exchange a chunk of our lives for money. Yet, are we getting value in this exchange? Are we even aware of this exchange? These are valid questions—whether we are acquiring money or spending it.

In some sense, that speaks to what we are doing to generate money more than it speaks to the money itself. Is that the question you are raising? Do we really need to look at what it is we are doing to get this money?

That's part of it. And the other part of it is, when we pay for something, we need to understand what we are paying with. Is this just a greenback, or is this a chunk of our life energy? And, as such, what's rippling out into the world out of our life energy? I think it's fundamental that all of us really want to contribute. Maybe I'm an idealist, but I think that is the most fundamental desire in each one of us.

So the question becomes: "When I part with my money, how am I making a contribution?" In the largest sense. After all, that money is a chunk of my life energy because some life energy went into acquiring it. So I'm putting a chunk of my life energy out into the world. Is it making a contribution? Furthermore, is it in alignment with what I say my values are? And this is a very important point: Are we spending and earning money in alignment with what we purport to be our values in life? I think too often that is not the case. We don't even consider it. We don't even think about it. That certainly was a big issue for me. In answering that, a whole new realm opens up, and we can begin to make conscious decisions around that process.

Let's take a hypothetical situation. If I'm against the destruction of the rain forest, for example, I don't want to do anything to perpetuate that destruction. When I start to investigate, however, I might find that the rain forest is being destroyed to create cattle ranches so that more cattle can be raised to provide beef for the rest of the world. That means I should be careful how many hamburgers I eat or spend my money on because that's helping to deplete the rain forest. Is that what you're getting at?

That is a small part of it. It's really much larger than that, in that it's more contextual. Maybe I can relate a better example. Recently, I was showing someone around the Olympic Peninsula in the Pacific Northwest. He was from the Midwest. We came across an area just off the road that was totally clear-cut, and from the back of the car this fellow responds with outrage. "How ugly and how terrible!" were his comments. And at that moment, I realized he was building a 4,000-square-foot house for him and his wife. Well, who creates those clear-cuts? It's not viciousness on the part of the logging companies. They don't stockpile the logs just to be nasty. Demand creates those clear-cuts. Are we among the demanders for that which is desecrating the earth? Or are we, in some way, putting ourselves on the line in determining how we are going to spend our life energy? Is our money going to be consistent with our values? It may not be as specific as the number of hamburgers, but it's a consciousness. It's a way of looking at the issues and asking, "Am I part of the problem, or am I part of the solution?" That's the bigger picture.

Are you suggesting that people shouldn't go out and buy houses?

That would help a lot. We have about 1.6 dwellings in this country for every family unit. People have second homes and so on. Furthermore, why do two people need to live in a house with 3,000 or 4,000 square feet? There are certain parts of the country that are moving toward cooperative housing and communal housing. This is very different from the movement in the sixties, but it is a valuable use of the planet's resources. And that's the bottom line. Anytime we spend money—or I'd say, most times—we consume resources. Finite resources. More and more, we are realizing how finite our resources are on this planet. It's a little hypocritical to be campaigning for this and that ecological thing while we are the ones consuming those resources and then creating the problems of waste and waste disposal.

What about the credit situation? A lot of people buy things on credit, particularly in the United States. We have a huge credit economy.

In my opinion, that's really the biggest problem facing America and the world right now. We can start to remedy this situation as individuals by burning our credit cards. We need to pay off our debt as fast as we can and stop thinking in terms of laying the burden on generations in the future, because many of us are not going to be able to pay off the debts we've acquired as a nation and as individuals. So we're passing that burden on to our kids. That's a wonderful heritage, a wonderful inheritance for our kids—whether it's the national deficit or our own personal debt burden.

I can hear someone saying, "Well, I've got this debt burden, but I also have life insurance that will pay it all off when I die, so my kids won't have that problem."

In certain cases, that may be true. But the fact is that in America we're spending a lot more than we earn. Our savings rate is among the smallest in the world. This works neither for individuals nor for society collectively. And what does it do in terms of conserving resources that are precious? We could really run the planet into the ground through the use of credit, and I think to some extent we have been doing that. It's a process we've got to stop.

Part of the psychology of it is that our generation, generally, has only experienced good times in this country. We have only experienced inflation. As a result, we seem to have the attitude that we'd better buy now because next year it's going to be more expensive. Most of us have not studied economics and do not know that capitalism is indeed a cyclical way of economic determination. We're going to have deflation. That's part of the cycle. To function as if we are always going to have inflation is to fail to understand how the economy works. It's not too dissimilar from the way that the Depression influenced the thinking of our parents in the fifties. They couldn't see good times when they were happening because they were expecting bad times. Similarly, we assume inflation is a way of life, and that we'd better stock up now because prices are going to be higher, so just spend. That ain't necessarily so.

What about something such as real estate? I heard the same argument 30 years ago about the real estate market—that it couldn't hold on any longer. But somehow it's held on.

It's amusing, but things usually last a lot longer than we think. Good cycles last a lot longer, and there have been plenty of warnings—especially in the last five years—that even real estate will have to go at some point. And, certainly, if we had bought some Houston real estate or some farmland in the Midwest, we'd be pretty sorry now. There's a very influential fellow, Stanley Salvigsen, who runs a large institutional advisory service basically in New York. He used to be the head man, or at least very high up, at Merrill Lynch. He has recently come out with a stunningly negative, and yet, in my opinion, very accurate perception of what is going to be happening. He calls it rolling depression, indicating that what we've seen in oil country and in the Midwest is only the beginning of this domino effect. Rather than it all coming down at once, it will come down one sector at a time. He feels that real estate will be one of those sectors that comes down very hard. It is difficult to come out with this kind of Cassandra or doomsday report when we are in the profession. During my ten years on Wall Street, I couldn't come out with something like that. I mean, it's un-American, it's heresy. When we get to the status of independent, as Salvigsen has recently, then we can speak out about that kind of thing.

It's as if the institutional or government authorities can't really tell the truth. I mean, if they said something negative, they could create a negative situation.

They would create a panic. But what I propose is that through fiscally sound processes, we can prevent that kind of calamity. We can place ourselves in a position where we can be part of the solution rather than part of the problem. Depression in this country could be a very positive thing. I know that sounds a little bit weird, but social change comes out of crisis. Every crisis creates an opportunity. And the inevitable rebalancing of the tensions in the economy could make people think about values other than materialism.

"Yuppiedom," for example, could evolve into something much more meaningful. I'm finding more and more references to service as a way of life. There has been recent research on the health-inducing aspects of service and the fulfillment that comes from service without concern for money. That could evolve, I think, to a very high degree—as it evolved in the '30s. Cooperation rather than cutthroat competition will be the new direction. Instead of keeping up with the Joneses, our concern will be "How can I help the Joneses?" That was a set of values that became very amplifying in the '30s. And I think we could see it again.

I'm intrigued by the concept of a depression being a positive thing. What could be the positive outcome of a depression?

For one thing, people would have more time to spend with their kids. There wouldn't have to be two-salary households. There couldn't be. People might have the opportunity to smell the flowers. They might have the opportunity to begin exploring other aspects of life than the compulsion to make more money. That in itself would be a very major step forward. For us to maintain the economy as it is now, we need to constantly consume more. And we complain about certain countries that aren't inspiring their populace to consume more to help maintain the economy. What's that doing to the earth? Another positive outcome of a depression would be a slowdown in terms of environmental degradation, by having to slow down the economy. There will have to be some dislocations, some suffering. I'm not happy about that, and I'm not suggesting that this is something that has to happen. I'm just saying that much can be learned from it, and much can be salvaged from it. It may be the necessary two-by-four that we need to begin to readjust our perspectives and our values.

What other positive steps can people take right now? We've mentioned credit. We should definitely, if not burn our credit cards, stop using them. What about people who have money in savings accounts? What would you recommend that people do with funds they have on hand? Where should they put them? In other words, what's going to be safe?

Certainly the safest investments according to a lot of experts in the United States today are U.S. Treasury Bonds and other government agency bonds. They allow us to lock in at the interest rates available today, and Treasury Bonds are as safe as the government is. There is the argument that says, "Well, what if the government collapses?" If the government collapses, our dollar bills will be worthless, also. They are from the same issuer; it's just a different maturity on the same bill. So unless we are going to become survivalists and stash years' worth of food someplace, I'd say invest in things such as long-term Treasury Bonds and other U.S. agency bonds.

What about things such as gold, silver, and precious metals?

I'm not partial to them. They are not interest bearing, for one thing. Part of the program I outline is to be able to live on the interest.

What about municipal bonds?

Their safety is dubious. Municipalities do fold up, and I think if we have bad enough economic conditions, a lot of municipalities will default on their funds. They are not as safe as Treasury Bonds. Keeping money in the bank is fine, too. There is bank insurance, but the return isn't as much as Treasury Bonds yield. There was some very popular advice some years back when I was on Wall Street that involved cutting out the intermediary. I think it applies here. We might as well go into bonds ourselves. A lot of the other places where we deposit our funds are doing so. And the difference between what the intermediaries pay us and what the bonds pay them is their profit. We might as well collect the profit ourselves.

You claim that by following your course, people can become financially independent in five years. How is that possible?

Well, why isn't it possible? Assuming that it is impossible, I think, is part of the prevailing mind-set. Let me put it this way: I know a lot of people who have done it, and that's how long it took me. All it means is being dedicated and having a real commitment to doing it. Most of us currently live on much more money than we need. It is very difficult to articulate this particular idea, but I'm going to try. It's what I call the fulfillment curve.

Early on in our lives, we begin to see that there is a direct correlation between the money we spend and the amount of fulfillment that we get. And it is accurate at those levels. In other words, we spend more money, and we get sufficient food. We spend more money, and we get sufficient shelter. We get sufficient clothing. For a while, it's pretty much a straight line—the more money spent, the more fulfillment. But at some point, that straight line begins to curve. When we get beyond the survival stage and beyond a modicum of comfort, the money we spend buys increasingly less in terms of fulfillment. We don't notice this because for so long we've had the attitude that if we spend more money, we get more fulfillment. At that point, the curve becomes a drop-off.

We spend huge amounts of money to get less fulfillment, and we don't even notice it. For example, we find ourselves spending all of our time maintaining that motor home—or some other high-ticket item—that we're only going to use two weeks out of the year, and we don't notice that our lives are being consumed by maintaining these things that were supposed to be giving us more fulfillment.

What we need to do is define what is enough for us in our lives. And by enough, I don't mean involuntary simplicity; I mean that peak of fulfillment before the line turns around. We will find that that particular point is much lower than we think. Our jobs pay a certain amount of money, and we feel we need that amount to survive. But by following the steps in the course, we may get to a place where we find that the maximum fulfillment is a quarter that amount—considerably lower. Where is that extra money going to go? Well, it's going to go into savings and into the programs and investments that will ultimately allow us to live at one-quarter the level of our income without having to work for the money.

There are a couple of catches here. First, we each need to determine our purpose in life. There's got to be something else we need to do other than make "gazingus pins" or "veeblefitzers." During the course, we begin to examine what it is we want to do with our lives. We pose the questions: "What's my purpose? Why am I here?" These questions are asked not just philosophically but in a very pointed way. We want a specific answer to the question: "Why am I getting up and going into the office?" In the process of answering, we begin to understand what it is we really want to do or be. Usually it involves being of service to others. And we find that it costs very little to share ourselves in that way.

What a lot of people realize when they reach financial independence is that it's costing them a lot less to live than before, but they are more fulfilled because they have so many new areas of fulfillment. For example, I don't go to movies, and it's not because I don't think movies are wonderful. It's because I have so many more exciting things to do. I often used to tell my audience that standing up there and talking to them was my vacation. It was a source of joy. And the other projects that I'm doing are also sources of joy for me. So I don't have to spend money on entertainment. Life becomes entertainment. Service becomes entertainment. That is how we begin to totally upset the old paradigm that we function under, and it makes it possible to become financially independent in a matter of five years. Five years is an arbitrary figure, but I have seen enough people become financially independent in five years to know that it's not an unrealistic figure. I've also known people who have done it in a couple of years because they simplified their lives enormously, and they were in the upper-wage scale.

I think another mind-set that exists in the culture is that we have to have a lot of money in order to be financially independent. It's usually in the millions. We think we need at least a million dollars to be financially independent. What do you think about that?

I think it's ridiculous. Absurd. There are now a couple of books out; and magazines such as *Changing Times, Money*, and *Forbes* that have looked at early retirement. Some of the figures quoted there are ridiculous, of course, but they've also quoted figures as low as $100,000. This is for their audiences who are not necessarily service-oriented or wanting to do anything other than leisure activities with their retirement days. If they are willing to talk about something as low as $100,000, we know it could be a lot lower than that.

In the course, each person determines this amount individually. We're not talking about a million dollars, and we're not talking about an arbitrary figure that is imposed from outside or from our imagination. We go through a step-by-step method of determining what that peak of fulfillment is for each person. What we usually come up with is a ridiculously low figure relative to what we were spending before—and no deprivation! The opposite actually occurs—more satisfaction because it is the peak of fulfillment. And then there is another factor that kicks in. When we do reach financial independence, we realize how much money it was taking to maintain our jobs. There is commuting time, the cost of the clothes we wear, the upkeep of the status car, and the cost of the large house we buy to impress the boss and our co-workers. All of that drops away. We don't need any of that! Some people say that 80 percent of their expenses dropped away when they became financially independent. That's the kind of thing that occurs. Again, this isn't theory or an abstraction. This is a step-by-step process that we evolve in our own lifetime. So I refuse to give flat figures; each person has to determine an amount for himself or herself. The process of making that determination is part of the awakening process, as well as part of the process of aligning our values. That's what ties it all together.

I think one of the most impressive things about your course is the idea that we account for every penny that we spend. What does that really mean? I don't think most of us really think about every penny that we spend and what we're spending it for.

In a way, it's unfortunate that that's what so many people remember about the course. There are other things that I'd rather have them remember. That part takes about four minutes out of an eight-hour program. But that's what people remember because it is so unusual in our generation.

There is so much talk about taking our power back. We take our power back in relationships, and certainly it's important to take our power back in terms of government and participating in the political process. But we've never thought about taking our power back in money. If our actions around money are totally automatic, so that the spending is just robotic behavior, who's got the power? The money or us? Obviously, the money does. We don't have the power. Therefore, it becomes necessary to take our power back. After all, if it is our life energy, as I previously suggested, what's it doing for taking our own life in our hands? That becomes a very powerful metaphor. The actual process of keeping tabs on every cent is useful. But it's also a metaphor for being aware of what it is that we are doing with our lives. I often say that maybe this is a Western person's meditation, just keeping tabs on our money.

If people try becoming financially independent and spend the next several years of their lives doing so, doesn't it take away from their being able to contribute to the planet, since they are going to be putting all their energy into trying to achieve this state?

That's a very common question. What I say is, I'd rather have a full-timer working with one of the projects that I work with than a part-timer. If a five- or even a ten-year investment of our lives now will eventually result in being free full time, it's worth it. At that point, we won't have to be thinking about where the money is coming from or anything of that sort. We can put ourselves wholeheartedly into a project.

At the New Road Map Foundation, we give all of our money away—all the net proceeds. There are no salaries and virtually no overhead involved in the production of the course because it's all done by volunteers. We approach groups and organizations and projects that we respect to offer them money. It's amazing to me the number of times that people have said, "No, no, no. I've taken your course, and I think it is wonderful. Please send me some of your financially independent people—some of the folks who are available full time for service. We need that a lot more than money."

Most of the folks who become financially independent want to contribute. That's the important thing. And it's not as if people who are working to become financially independent are oblivious of the needs of the environment. Even while they remain part of the workforce, they are learning skills, doing values clarification, and preparing themselves for the future. Right in this area there are a lot of folks who are working with organizations such as Beyond War or the Seva Foundation, but their main focus right now is freeing themselves up so they can contribute more of their time later.

What about people who really enjoy making money? There are such people. They are really into making money, and they really enjoy making money. How would you convince them that there is something else they should do?

I think the operative word there is *should.* There are no *shoulds*. If people really enjoy what they're doing, I presume that they are making their contribution the way they need to be. I don't mean to imply that I'm judgmental and that everyone should drop what they're doing and start serving the planet. It would be useful and helpful, and I think Gaia, Mama Earth, needs all the help she can get at this point, but people have different skills, and if someone's skill lies in making money, that's fine. Making money generates a lot of jobs, and we need that, too.

To stretch the point a little further, we might also ask: "What if somebody is enjoying his or her work and feels that he or she is serving the planet through that work? Why would that person want to achieve financial independence?" The answer to that is freedom—the freedom from having to take money for a job. I've gotten so many letters from people saying, "I was a schoolteacher, and

I loved being a schoolteacher, but I felt constrained. I couldn't buck the bureaucracy; I couldn't teach the way I wanted to teach because I'd be out of a job." But the moment that they achieved financial independence, they said, "I can do it my way. I can be creative, and I don't have to have this sword of Damocles over my head, worrying that if I do things differently I'll be fired." Once people are free of having to take money for a job, their creative output is phenomenal.

That's just one factor, and I think there are more. One of my favorite quotes is: "We can't serve two masters, God and Mammon"—Mammon being the material world. I think that has a very deep effect on us. When we are doing something purely for love, purely because we want to be doing it, and there is no concern whatsoever for a paycheck, we pull out all the stops. There is no burnout—even working 120 hours a week. Other people—those working just for the paycheck—get burnt out in 40-hour-a-week jobs. If that's not the case, nothing is lost. I'm not suggesting that every person on this planet has to go out and become financially independent, but I think a lot of people can be, and I think it can be very beneficial to the entire planet.

If you could only tell people one or two things about how they could improve their relationship with money, what would you tell them?

The first thing I would tell people would be to clear up their debt. The second thing I would tell them is to be aware of how money is flowing in their lives. I think those would be the two most important things I could say. Take money seriously because it is part of you. And possibly a third thing I would say is: "Don't buy into the idea that you have to work at making a living all your life. There may be more important things to do. Prepare for the discovery of that." One of the best ways to help discover what is important is by taking this course—or by doing anything else that puts you in a position to open up your consciousness.

The phrase "making a living" is interesting. It implies that somehow we have to "make" a living, when we are really just living.

I often substitute "making a dying" for that phrase, because I don't see people coming back from their jobs more alive than when they left in the morning. I see them much deader. I concluded a long time ago that working for a paycheck was much closer to "making a dying." Certainly, the high numbers of job-related illnesses, such as high blood pressure and heart attack, make the phrase "making a dying" all too true.

In a profound sense, what we are really talking about is how we can live more richly, learning to take control of our lives in a way we haven't done before.

Exactly.

※ ※ ※

EPILOGUE

In a lucid and refreshing way, Joe Dominguez cuts through the "stuff" around money and provides several practical insights into how we can improve our relationship to money. Not the least of these is the link between our consumption patterns and the use of limited and finite resources. This is a particular problem for those of us who live in the United States, where we consume one-third of the world's resources. The only way to change this overconsumption is for each of us to become more aware and transform our personal buying habits, which also relates to how we use credit, as Dominguez states. He also expresses the importance of service as a way of life and how financial independence affords a level of freedom that gives us the opportunity to contribute time and energy to worthwhile activities, at the same time enhancing meaning and purpose in our life.

The essential message of Dominguez' approach is that we have the power to choose how we are with money. It is possible to make a life while making a living instead of "making a dying."

⁂ ⁂ ⁂ ⁂ ⁂ ⁂

CHAPTER THREE

The Soul of Money

Lynne Twist and Michael Toms

PROLOGUE

Money. Much misunderstood in our culture. And much maligned. It can be a vehicle for personal and social transformation, yet it is rarely seen from this perspective. Money can be a vehicle for love, energy, intention, clarity, commitment, and vision—from the highest aspirations and ideals. The personal relationship we have with money determines how it functions in our lives. Many of us have wounds around money that keep us stuck and prevent money from flowing naturally through our lives. There is a new context for money based on sufficiency and wholeness. And this serves as the focus of this dialogue with Lynne Twist. She is a founding executive of the Hunger Project, an international not-for-profit organization dedicated to ending chronic, persistent hunger worldwide. Ms. Twist's leadership of the Hunger Project has been an important factor in the project's growth and development. Over the past two decades, more than 6.5 million people in more than 150 countries have enrolled in the Hunger Project, and Hunger Project staff and volunteers cur-

rently conduct ending-hunger activities in more than 35 countries worldwide.

Ms. Twist has traveled extensively in both the developed and developing world and has addressed tens of thousands of individuals and organizations with respect to the issue of ending hunger. She is the director of Strategic Funding for the Hunger Project, serves on the Board of Directors of the Institute of Noetic Sciences, is a trustee of the Fetzer Institute, and is co-chairman of the board of the State of the World Forum. Ms. Twist has served as an advisor and consultant to numerous global and not-for-profit entities and serves on the global commission to fund the United Nations. She was honored in 1994 as a woman of distinction at the United Nations by the International Health Awareness Network.

With Lynne Twist's guidance, we will explore the depth and breadth of money, what it means to us, and how we can understand it in a way that will lead to a more fulfilling life.

❋ ❋ ❋

MICHAEL TOMS: *You offer workshops and seminars on what's called the "Soul of Money," and we don't ordinarily connect the words* soul *and* money. *How do you do that, and why do you that?*

LYNNE TWIST: It's my experience that money is an inanimate object that we made up. It has no power or authority other than what we assign to it. And we can assign to it a kind of spiritual meaning, voice, and power, if we choose to, and give it some soul. It doesn't have any, but we do. And we are the people through whom money flows and with whom money speaks. When I talk about the soul of money, what I really mean is your soul and my soul and how to use money as another avenue to express the soulful human beings that we are. I see money a little bit like water. When water is moving and flowing, it cleanses, purifies, creates growth, and makes things green and beautiful. When it starts to slow down and is held still, it becomes stagnant and toxic. I think that is true of money as well.

Those of us who have a hard time letting money flow—flow through our lives and to our highest commitments—sometimes get a little cloudy on the topic. It's like looking through a toxic fish tank out into the world: You can't see clearly. You begin to horde it and accumulate it as if it belongs to you. Money flows around the world through all of our lives. It doesn't belong to anybody—it belongs to everybody. One of my missions, I think, is to enable people to keep money flowing, and in doing that, to empower people to assign money to fulfill their highest commitments and ideals, to send it off into the universe and into the world with love, with voice, with commitment, and with vision. I think money can carry that energy with it wherever it goes. Conversely, I think that when we send money off with resentment and with some sort of defensive feelings—such as when we pay our taxes, and we're angry about it and try to cheat—all that negative energy goes with the money. That kind of negative energy goes with the money into our government, so we spend it on defense and on congressmen accusing each other of cheating or unethical behavior and other things that are wasteful. Our government actually has money that is not as pure and blessed as it could be if we consciously invested our money in the government of the United States or any country where you pay taxes. This is what I mean about imbuing money with soul.

In terms of taxes, many people never actually send money to the government. They just have it taken out of their paychecks. In some ways, it's not so conscious. Still, there is a feeling that somehow we are paying more money to the government than we should be. Or it's going for the wrong things—or whatever. How are consciousness and intention related?

I consider fund-raising really holy work. Some people think fund-raising is a drag, a necessary evil, and they try to avoid it whenever they can. I relish and luxuriate in the privilege of asking people for money, and I bring, I hope, a new light and joy to it. I feel that we all need to re-source our relationship with money. It has a huge influence over our lives. Whether you are living in India and have two or three rupees to your name, or you're a multibillionaire living in Santa Monica on the beach, or anyone in between, money deeply influences our lives. We've let it master us. We've let it rule us. We need to re-source our relationship with money—which is an invention, something we made up—and actually "sourcefully" authorize our money to pay taxes. Then, instead of just being upset because the government took it from us, right out of our paycheck, we would actually see that we are *investing* in roads, schools, educational programs for our young people, environmental programs, the federal park system—the things we need to have a safe, secure life. If we could remember that our taxes are a way of "vesting ourselves" in and taking responsibility for the governance of our nation and our world—we could make our relationship with the government, the United Nations, and all governance much more fulfilling, much more responsible.

When we can re-source or re-think our relationship with money, we can see it as our voice: our voice for change; our voice for transformation; our voice for a more loving, more peaceful, more compassionate, more sustainable world. It's not our vote. I'm saying it's our voice. We can actually speak with our money, especially in an affluent society. When money gets involved, people take you seriously—until then it's all talk. Money has no inherent power, but it has the power that we give it. If I were holding an Italian lira in front of you and you didn't know the exchange rate, it would not mean anything to you until someone explained what the exchange rate was. Or if I were holding a taka from Bangladesh, it would mean nothing to you, but to a Bangladeshi, it would mean everything. This illustrates that money only has the meaning we assign to it. The meaning lives with us; it doesn't live with money. And in my view, we've overassigned meaning to money.

It seems to me that we've made money, in many cases, more important than human life; we've made it more important than God. And at the heart of that is a real lie that we are telling about money, a lie that has people killing for money, doing terrible things to their own children for money. I've never run across anyone who hasn't been hurt by his or her relationship with money. It's a raw area, an open wound, because all of us have done something we really aren't proud of to move more money in our direction. There is a lot of healing to be done around this topic and around our relationship with money. Fund-raising and philanthropy can be an arena where we begin to heal this relationship with money. People can begin to see that they can "author" money, reinvent it for themselves, and move it toward their highest commitments rather than have it sort of seduced from them for their basest desires.

That's a hard concept to relearn. The advertising community appeals to our basest desires. We are bombarded with messages telling us that we are not whole until we buy this product, that we are not beautiful until we use this on our hair. There is something wrong with the way we smell until we put on this perfume or aftershave. We're told we are not whole, we're not complete, we're not sufficient. We receive these messages 24 hours a day. And we need to make up for that deficiency by buying something.

I'm suggesting that we adopt a whole different ground of being, a whole different base, which is that we *are* whole and complete already. We are sufficient exactly the way we are. And one way of expressing that is to invest our money and give voice to our money to fulfill the highest ideals that match the wholeness of human life and the wholeness of who we all are. To me, that is a new relationship with money, a fulfilling relationship with money—a way for money to express and carry the message of love.

One of the common aspects around money seems to be that we don't have enough of it. We always want more. And as we look around, particularly in American culture, we see Michael Jordan signing for $25 million a year or a football player turning down a $30 million contract. The money is so gigantic. How much is enough? What is enough? What about that question? The enough question—how much money is enough?

That question is right at the heart of the lie or the breakdown in integrity in our relationship with money. Money is like a lightning rod for what I call the lie or the myth of scarcity. We don't just think things are scarce. We think from a "condition of scarcity." We have a mind-set, or a frame of reference, that no matter what's happening, there is not enough. Picture yourself going through a day. When you wake up in the morning, no matter what time you went to bed and no matter what time you wake up, the first thought you have is, *I didn't get enough sleep.* And the next thought you have is, *I don't have enough time to get myself to work on time,* or *There's not enough milk in the refrigerator,* or *We don't have enough money to do the things we want.* If you are running a volunteer organization, there aren't enough volunteers. If you are running a profit-making organization, there aren't enough profits. It seems to be the frame of reference for life, particularly in the industrialized affluent societies, but it is pretty much that way all over the planet.

No matter whom you talk to, you can get agreement and you can get a whole conversation going about "There isn't enough this" and "I don't have enough that." It's a frame of reference for the way we live and think. Money is the great lightning rod for this scarcity belief in almost any society. I'm suggesting that we rethink all of that—particularly, at this time in history, when we are facing environmental challenges beyond what any generation has seen before. We need to start noticing and taking responsibility and authoring a context of *sufficiency*, of wholeness, of completeness, of integrity, and let me say again, *sufficiency*. Not abundance. I believe that *abundance* is the flip side of scarcity. It's having more than you need. Scarcity is not having enough or having less than you need. Sufficiency is having exactly what you need. If we really look around and look into our lives, authentically, clearly, we see that we have *exactly* what we need. We know the glass is exactly full—not almost full or over full. And living a life with the recognition and responsible space of sufficiency is a very fulfilling life, but it's a context one must call forth and create.

There is something I call the principle of sufficiency, and it is: *If you let go of what we are trying to get more of (which is what we are all trying to get more of), it frees up oceans of energy to make a difference with what you have. When you make a difference with what you have, it expands.* I'm talking about love, I'm talking about time, I'm talking about relatedness. I'm even talking about money. If we sit down and make a difference with the money that we have, we will find that it expands. We have an experience of wealth. Or if we look, we can make a difference with the time we have each day—really make a difference with it, and it expands. We've all had the experience of going through a day that was so productive, so exciting that it seemed like it was a month long. And when we go to bed at night, we can't even remember all the way back to the morning. That's a day that made a difference. When we make a difference with our lives, with our time, with our relationships, with our love, with our money, it expands. And we don't have that focus on scrambling to get more of what we don't really need, which is what we're so busy doing that we don't even notice who we are and what we have. The context of sufficiency is making a difference with who we are, what we have, and knowing that it's whole, complete, and exactly enough. This context is not a set of circumstances, but a declaration, a place to stand, a way of being and living, and it creates a life of fulfillment and contribution.

This sounds like understanding in ourselves the difference between wants and needs. There are a lot of things that we want but we may not need. So, it's really getting clear about those two things, isn't it?

Yes, and it's a very timely inquiry for humanity, because most of our wants have become needs without our realizing it. For example, we think that we can't survive without more oil, without more land, without more cities, without more freeways. Some people can't survive without another cigarette, some without another pair of shoes, or whatever it is. Some of it is small. Some of it is large. And by turning our wants and our desires into needs, we've created another myth, another lie, at the base of a culture that is out of control. It's a myth that is addictive, consumptive, and in which we are really, truly lost.

As a fund-raiser, I have the great privilege, since I work on hunger and poverty, to interact with many, many people who have very little. Some of our Hunger Project on-the-ground programs are in places like Bangladesh, India, Ghana, or Senegal. Interacting with people in these countries, I see in their faces and in their communal way of life with their children and their elders a kind of satisfaction and fulfillment that is missing in our society. We have a hunger, but ours is not physical; it's a hunger for meaning, for connection, for belonging, for more validation that we are okay. The whole concept of wants becoming needs is a function of just being unclear about who we are. It is a symptom of having lost our spiritual base, our connectedness with one another, and with the earth itself. This survival grip that scarcity has on us has us behaving in a kind of insane way. We really are out of control. This is a time of great challenge and stress.

We live in a free market economy of capitalism. One aspect of this type of economy is that we want to create more goods. Progress is based on growth, and that's like creating more wants. It's an endless cycle. So, we really need to look at our whole economic base, don't we?

Yes, we do, and fortunately there are many people looking at these issues from this perspective. My work is more on the personal level because I think the outer world is a reflection of our inner truth. I think inner work, particularly at this time, is very important. It's easy to have compassion for the poor, but it's really hard to have compassion for the rich. I have found that the vicious cycle of wealth is as intractable as the vicious cycle of poverty. People seem to be more familiar with and more interested in—and I put myself in this category—intervening in the vicious cycle of poverty. But we must remember—and Mother Teresa has been a great mentor to me in this regard—that the vicious cycle of wealth is what has the whole planet going down an unsustainable track.

It isn't just very, very rich people who are going down this track; it's people like us who live in affluent societies. We become trapped in a mind-set, and once we start making a little bit more money than we need, we start acquiring things—things that we really don't need. We begin to buy into the notion that we must have the next car, the next house, the next vacation. Then, we have to take care of these things. It reaches a point where being able to contribute money or invest in a better world becomes almost impossible because we have to maintain all these belongings and extras that we've accumulated. We have to maintain them because these acquisitions have come to define who we are. We actually believe that we *are* our homes, our cars, our bank accounts. And this is, in my view, the vicious cycle of wealth that is part of an affluent culture and a market economy. If we can break away from that, on an individual basis, we can begin to dismantle the great structures that are driving us in an unsustainable, cataclysmic direction that I think we are all wanting to do something about.

What are some of the ways we can break this destructive pattern? Do you have any suggestions?

One way we can begin to break away from that kind of thinking is to invest our money in not-for-profit work. When we take a stand for a better world with our money, we're saying, "This is who I am, this is what I stand for, and this is my voice." My husband and I, for example, have given more than a million dollars to the Hunger Project over the years, and we don't have a million dollars sitting around. We are not rich people. But we have allowed this commitment to end hunger to shape who we are and keep us centered in service. Our goal is to leave this planet better than we found it and to build a sustainable future for our children, our grandchildren, and all future generations. We want our checkbook to reflect those things. Most people can look in their checkbook and find out exactly what they are committed to because it's right in there. And if you record faithfully in your checkbook (and the bank does if you don't), you will see what you are committed to.

In our society, money is the voice of our commitment. My great quest and my great privilege is to ask people for money every day of my life. I invite people to move the money that flows through their life toward their highest ideals of commitment. And it's a joy to do so because it is an intimate and deep interaction with the hearts and souls of others. I can offer them a way to take their money, which seems so far from the soul, and bring it into the very heart and breadth and depth of their being. I want to show them that money can be part of their self-expression. I want to let people know that the money that flows around the planet—which really belongs to none of us, or belongs to all of us—can begin to be allocated to our highest commitments. People can be known for what they allocate, rather than what they accumulate. When we are known for what we allocate, what we invest in, rather than what we accumulate, that's when society will be sustainable.

Wealth is often equated with money, and yet, wealth really is much more than just having money, isn't it? What is wealth to you?

Wealth—or another word we might use is *prosperity*—is a sense of joy and creativity and fulfillment in life. If people have that, they don't label it wealth. But we could start doing that. And that doesn't take money. Every morning the sun comes up and lights up the sky no matter where we live. And when we sit and watch the sunset, we realize the wealth, prosperity, and well-being that is available all around us—in our relationship with the earth, the sun, the solar system, and the stars. Wealth is understanding the beauty and magnificence of a tree. Wealth is being in love with your husband, your wife, your work. Wealth lies in the joy of raising a child. This is wealth in my book, and it costs nothing. That kind of wealth is an investment of the human spirit. And when our human spirit is unleashed, what's unleashed is prosperity of the soul, prosperity of the heart—an experience of love, relatedness, and inner-connectedness. We experience the deep truth that we are each other, and in that truth, the whole world belongs to us.

Buckminster Fuller's philosophy was that there was enough to go around, that we had enough resources to feed the whole planet right now. I don't think that's changed since his death in 1983. I think it's still true. I think an important point that we have yet to really understand and realize is that the priorities we set determine what happens. With that in mind, we have to reexamine our priorities. Do you agree?

Deepak Chopra says that you are where you put your attention. You are your attention. I completely agree with that. Because money plays such a gigantic role in our lives, we are either denying it (people who are in the poverty-consciousness racket), or we are scrambling to get more of it. We focus so much consciousness on money. If we just transform that one aspect of our life and our world, it would be such a revolution—such an evolution—of humanity. I feel that this is one of the great places to go to work. It's a place where people have skeletons in their closet. It's a place where everyone's done something bad. Maybe they stole a quarter out of their grandmother's purse when they were six, and they've never forgiven themselves. Maybe they shoplifted when they were in the fifth grade. Or maybe they made an investment that turned out to be a scam, and they are embarrassed about it. Everybody has these kinds of dark corners about money. So I like to go into the den of money, the Lion's Den, with a big spotlight, and give people an opportunity to clean it out, clear it out, to author, take ownership, forgive themselves, and then bring money into the light.

We need to bring money into the light because all good things need to be paid for. This is what it takes to make something happen. That's the way we've got ourselves organized, so let's use our money to make things happen that nurture, that bring light to the planet, that transform, that inspire, that uplift. Let's use our money in that way rather than using it to go see, for example, some of these movies that are so violent, so depressing, so dark. When you walk out of the theater, you think, *Why did I spend my money and my time exposing myself to that horror?* Yet, these are big box-office successes. Our money is feeding some of the deepest, darkest parts of our society and what I'll call a learning curve that's going down instead of up. We can turn that around the minute we want. Money has immense power because we've said so; now let's give it the power that the universe, humanity, the earth, and the planet needs at the end of the 20th century. Let's use money, the very thing that people think is so evil, to bring in the light, to transform the future, to end hunger and poverty, and to fund consciousness research.

Where we put our attention creates the world around us. We are so trained by advertising. The average American youngster watches about four or five hours of television a day. Most adults watch even more. There are some wonderful things on television, but much of television consists of bombarding us with the kind of messages that take us down. These messages train us to have spending habits that don't serve us, get us into debt, and encourage us to buy things we don't want and don't need.

We must develop spending habits and practices that further our commitments. I'm talking about philanthropy now. Everyone can be a philanthropist, and I think everyone is. If we can all start using those practices instead of buying the next whatever it is that we buy every day, we would really have a different world. Things are shaped by that bottom line whether we like it or not. The rain forests will continue to be cut down unless they are more valuable standing than cut—economically valuable. We need to be able to prove these things to ourselves and to a market economy.

I think it's important to promote philanthropy and fund-raising in all kinds of places. I've gone up to homeless people who've been asking me for money, and I've asked them for money. Whenever I see a homeless person, I know that what they really want is to make a difference and to be loved and known. So instead of giving them something, I take their hand. I give them a hug. I talk to them about the Hunger Project. I talk to them about the people I know in Ethiopia. And I give them the sense of how much opportunity they have in their life and how many gifts they've received from the people who've walked by them. I do what I can to have them really take full advantage of the great spirit that we have available to us in America to make something of ourselves and to contribute to the world, rather than be somebody who's taking.

We really have an opportunity at this time in history to take this thing called money and make it one of the most powerful instruments for the transformation of the world. That is part of what I personally am working on and hope more people will join me in working on. The great joy of my life is in asking people for money. I see it as holy, blessed work, because when you raise money the way I'm talking about, the money has a blessed feel to it. It's "sourceful," blessed money, and it carries with it that karma, that beauty, that energy, that light.

We are wealthy in many, many ways. Resources and money. And yet we do have homeless; we do have people who are hungry; and we do have children who are malnourished, underfed, and undereducated. That's a reflection of our unconsciousness around money, isn't it?

It's almost like when someone is knocking at the door for guidance, for assistance, for partnership, and you don't hear them knock, then they knock harder. And then when you don't hear them knock, they break your door down. And then when you don't see them, they park themselves right in front of you. And I'm talking in consciousness terms. In America, as generous as we've been, we've been patronizing with our generosity. In many cases, we haven't created a partnership. We've been charitable in a way that has not enabled people's dignity. Therefore, right here in the midst of our own wealthy, affluent, unbelievably rich society, we have poverty; we have people who are uneducated; we have illiteracy; we have all the problems that we thought we were keeping out there, far away from us. They are right here, now. They are in our face. If I refer to it in terms of consciousness, it is kind of like beating us over the head. We've got to change the direction in which we are going. We are just off course. We all know that we are, now. This is not a mystery. But to change course takes some real commitment and some real integrity, rather than getting what you can before the whole thing is gone. I see the area of money to be once again the critical, central thing driving us in the wrong direction, until we re-relate to money.

In my work as a fund-raiser, I've seen massive, deep, profound transformation in people's lives that would just make you weep. People who have had no real sense of their ability to give thousands of dollars have found ways to rearrange their lives to do that, to invest their money in something like ending chronic, persistent hunger. Or they give money to the Institute of Noetic Sciences where consciousness research and really important studies are going on. In the act of giving money, they find their own wealth and wholeness. It's not before. It is in that act of sharing. In that action of expression with money, they find wholeness, sufficiency, and the depth of their own integrity.

In my own work, I have needed to define in myself where I lack compassion. I'm a loving person, and, I think, a compassionate person. Where I start losing my compassion is when I'm dealing with the very wealthy. The wealthier the person, the harder it is for me to deal with them because they seem so isolated and so distant to me. I think my karma this time around is to bring the same compassion and love to the extremely rich that I can bring to the extremely poor. That's one of the great lessons I've learned in fund-raising and in the Hunger Project, but it's always a challenge for me.

One of the stories about you is that you raised a million dollars from ten people who gave $100,000 each, and you took them to Bangladesh after they'd given the money to show them where their money was going. That's a very compelling story.

This is a regular activity of mine. I don't really show donors where their money went because I am not a proponent of the rich giving to the poor, or the "haves" giving to the "have nots." The opportunity of the trips is for people from two completely different cultures to form a co-equal partnership for a better world. I've trained fund-raisers in Bangladesh, which is the second poorest country in the world. I've trained fund-raisers in Africa in places where people don't think they have any money. I say that ten rupees from an Indian child on the streets of Bombay invested in ending hunger has as much power as $500,000 from Ted Turner or someone like him. When you go to the bank, you don't get that message from the bank. But I'm saying that money, if it's raised with integrity and intentionality, carries the relationship of the donor to their money. That is what gives money its power. So the 50 rupees can truly buy as much or more of the end of hunger than $50,000 or $500,000 given as a "gesture."

These people who go on the trips have given $100,000 or $300,000 or $1 million and obviously have a pretty affluent life, a pretty comfortable life. I take them on journeys to meet their co-equal partners in the villages of the developing world, and they bond. They see that they are each other. It is not a case of rich people helping poor people. It is that they *are each other*. If you were born in a Bangladesh village instead of in Sausalito or New York or wherever you were born, you see by being with your brothers and sisters in Bangladesh that it would take real courage to do as well as the people that you will meet there. In fact, you have enormous respect for them from then on. You will never feel sorry for them; you will not want to "help" them. You will want to learn from them, be their partner, be their colleague, and together hold hands and build a better world in full partnership.

These trips are unbelievably transformational for people. They never forget them. And sometimes I take people who have traveled everywhere. If they have a lot of money, they can go wherever they want. But never like this. We sleep in the villages. We get our hands in the dirt with the farmers. We sit in meditation with some of the village elders. Whether it's in India, Bangladesh, Ghana, or Senegal, we dance with the women, and we beat the drums with the drummers. This is real bonding. There's no tourism in this. There is no learning "about cultures." It is about becoming one with someone whose life is so different from yours, yet in their heart and in their soul, all they want is what you want: to love and be loved, to make a difference with their life, to live a life of dignity and wholeness. And that's what I want. That's what you want. And we see that no matter what, we are each other. We are in this together. And that's how we are going to get out of it—by holding hands together and building, creating, authoring, and investing in a better world.

Even the people in the villages of Ghana invest in the Hunger Project. So we are all on the donor rolls. There are no recipients. We don't have any recipients. In fact, although I've traveled to most of the developing world, I've never met a needy person. I've only met self-reliant, self-sufficient, dignified human beings who are in some way prevented by cultures, systems, and structures from expressing their natural gifts. This whole arena of taking people from the affluent societies to the poor societies has been a tremendous experience for me and for the people who participate. Another thing we've learned is that the people from these resource-poor nations such as Bangladesh are not aiming to create an affluent society any longer. They see that affluence causes deep problems. They see mental illness growing in affluent societies. They see divorce and breakdown of families. They see crime; they see a kind of separateness and isolation. They don't want that—and thank God they don't. So they, in partnership with us (who've made those mistakes), will find a new way of living, a new kind of human being, a new kind of economy, a new kind of society. There are 5.8 billion of us, and 80 percent of all of us on Earth live in developing countries. It will take the voice of that 80 percent to find the new way of living and being that will be sustainable.

These partnerships are very important, and even if it's just a handful of people, miracles come out of it. The trips are really wonderful. They are powerful, and they are for people who are already committed to investing money. I don't take people who are just curious, because it dishonors the people we visit. I take people who are invested, very committed to invest, or vested in building a new future for humanity. The people we visit know that the donors are serious because they've put their money on the table. And that's how you say you're serious in our society.

What is the money that is donated to the Hunger Project actually used for?

The money is used to provide training, empowerment, strategic planning, and transformation. With Hunger Project training, people can create environments in which their self-sufficiency and self-reliance can be fully expressed and unleashed. They begin to see how to remove those roadblocks around them. Whether it's that they can't get a loan from a government official or because moneylenders have a grip on the village or because they need a bridge to sell their goods, they learn how to see a way through. It's not that the Hunger Project pays for the bridge or buys out the moneylenders or bribes the official. It's that the Hunger Project empowers people to work within what are seemingly intractable situations in partnership with people in all sectors of their society through something called "Strategic Planning and Action" and create breakthroughs.

We empower people and build relationships that are missing. We empower them to rethink entrenched structures and systems and transform them so they can have healthy, productive lives. In southern India, for example, in the state of Tamil Nadu, near Madras, there has long been a practice of female infanticide. The people of this area are very poor. A man's worth is measured by the number of sons he has rather than by any monetary currency. What that means is that pregnant women hope and pray they have a boy baby instead of a girl. If a woman has a girl, she is sometimes so ashamed that she will smother her baby daughter, or she'll get the midwife or a sister to help kill the baby right after she's born. The women feel that what they are doing is kind because a woman's life is so hard in this part of the world. They feel it's better not to have her live. Even though she has somehow, in her way, made it logical and right and rational to do this horrible thing, still when a mother kills her child, she is deeply traumatized. Hunger Project monies were invested in Tamil Nadu to launch a campaign to put an end to female infanticide.

Some of the work we've done in Tamil Nadu involves holding awareness camps for women who have killed their children. We have facilitators and animators who create an environment where these women can share the horror of what they've done so they can forgive themselves. Once they forgive themselves, they can stop doing it, they stop assisting other women in doing it, and the whole entrenched system begins to break apart and disappear.

Another part of the campaign to stop female infanticide involved making a public service announcement (PSA). We were able to get the most well-known male and female cinema stars in India (they happen to be married to each other) to donate their time to make a PSA. It runs before and after every movie in Tamil Nadu, and everybody goes to the movies. This PSA is about 60 seconds long and tells the story of the birth of the celebrity couple's baby. The PSA briefly depicts the pregnancy, the wife's hospitalization and labor, and the husband's trip to the hospital. When he arrives at the hospital, he is told he has a daughter. In a series of quick scenes, the film shows the father holding this beautiful baby girl, and then he's bathing her, and she's three or four years old. She's then shown at 17 and in school, and a few seconds later she's an adult in her 30s or 40s and obviously a lawyer. Finally, the film shows her taking groceries to her elderly parents, taking care of them in their old age. In 60 seconds, the film shows that girls do have value, they are useful, and they are important to society. This PSA has been distributed all over the state of Tamil Nadu and has helped reshape how the state's 55 million people think about women and female infants.

A third component of the campaign is a pop song that plays on the radio in India and talks about the value of girls. This female infanticide problem and practice is gradually disappearing as a result of this media campaign and the awareness camps all provided by Hunger Project[1] money.

That's one of dozens of projects in India that have been implemented by the Indian people to improve their quality of life. These things cost very little, but they revolutionize the thinking of millions of people and transform the very quality and meaning of life for all.

EPILOGUE

The ideas that Lynne Twist espouses provide a new ground of being around money. Her emphasis on giving, compassion, generosity of spirit, and spiritual integrity relative to "allocating" money in place of accumulating it, sets a creative model to emulate. She also speaks of separating who we are from our money or what our money has acquired for us. One senses a palpable joy and aliveness coming from Lynne as she redefines wealth in terms of the human spirit. How we are with our money also falls under her scrutiny as she suggests taking back our power and directing our money to socially relevant and beneficial projects that serve people and the planet.

Perhaps the most profound aspect of what Lynne Twist has to tell us is the reality that we can discover our own wholeness and learn what true wealth means through investing money in a worthwhile endeavor. It is a privilege to be able to give, and in the process of giving, we receive an even greater gift of self-discovery in return.

❋ ❋ ❋ ❋ ❋ ❋

[1] You may reach the Hunger Project at 15 E. 26th St., New York, NY 10010; or by telephone at (212) 532-9100.

CHAPTER FOUR

Principles of Prosperity

C. Holland Taylor and Michael Toms

PROLOGUE

Economics is usually the domain of economists, politicians, and bureaucrats who spout forth an endless stream of statistics, percentages, and jargon that only serves to confuse anyone concerned enough to listen. For the most part, we try to muddle through our own economic maze in spite of the rhetoric, doing the best we can to keep it together on the financial level and hoping the whole system doesn't crash around us, although we frequently see ourselves economically as reluctant passengers on a sinking Titanic. Is there a way through the eye of the needle? Perhaps there is. Especially if you follow the advice given in a highly touted book entitled The Prosperity Handbook. *In the following dialogue, co-author C. Holland Taylor unravels the economic riddle for us, and in the process, brings some light to the dark corners of our personal money maze.*

⁂

MICHAEL TOMS: *Your book used to be called* The Money Bible. *Why did the title change to* The Prosperity Handbook?

HOLLAND TAYLOR: We like to think that the book is an authoritative guide to achieving financial and personal success. With that in mind, we thought that referring to the book as *The Money Bible* would be appropriate, but then we realized that a lot of people don't like to hear an association made between money and the Bible. It is almost profane. So we switched to *The Prosperity Handbook* because that's another way of expressing what we are communicating in this book.

How did you get involved in such a project?

Several years ago, right after President Reagan was elected, we had double-digit inflation; we were about to enter the worst recession since the 1930s, and the state of the economy was a headline story day after day, month after month, year after year. Yet, very few of us understood what was going on in the economy. We didn't know what to do to protect ourselves, what to do to change our society so that we would not be faced with this type of problem again, and there was nowhere we could turn for this type of information. What I wanted to do was make this information readily available. So I researched what experts were saying and then began applying spiritual principles to the economic problems that were confronting our country.

When I researched the experts, I found that there was a lot of disagreement among them, but there was also a strain of consistency throughout in terms of fundamental facts that govern our economy. These facts are not readily available. There are not many books out there written in simple terms that explain what's going on. Take the issue of inflation, for example. If you look in the dictionary, you'll find inflation defined as an increase in the supply of money, which is usually followed by higher prices. It is hard for anybody to disagree that when the government prints more money, it makes the money of elderly Americans who are on a fixed income worth less. It decreases the purchasing power of someone who is earning a salary but whose salary does not keep up with inflation. So you have an obvious problem and an obvious solution to the problem as well, and that's the type of information that I wanted to get out. Inflation is not an act of God; it is an act of man. It takes place for specific reasons—because certain people benefit from inflation, and others are victimized by it. It is not the kind of thing that we want to see continuing in our society.

When one looks at the economic system, even if one isn't familiar with economics, one can quickly see that the system, the institutions, are really controlled by a few power brokers, and in some sense, inflation is also controlled by those same power brokers. Individuals can feel powerless in the midst of such seeming strength. What can individuals do against such power?

First of all, by having knowledge of what's going on, we can protect ourselves as individuals financially. If we know that the Federal Reserve inflates the money supply, we can take a portion of our savings and invest it in something that the Federal Reserve cannot manipulate, such as gold. In addition, the research that I've done over a period of years has clearly indicated to me that we have concentrated power in this country. The reason it continues to exist is because the average American is uninformed and doesn't know what to do about it, or if he is informed, he feels helpless. It is basically an abdication on the part of the average American citizen and voter that allows this process to continue. If enough Americans were educated on this issue, we'd be able to vote changes into effect. I wrote *The Prosperity Handbook* not only to provide us with the ability to protect ourselves financially, but to show what is going on so that people are empowered to make changes. I'm less interested in pointing to the people who are causing problems than I am in pointing to solutions. If we can implement solutions, the people who are causing the problems will be removed as a matter of course.

In the summer of 1984, in the state of California, the state supreme court voted down a proposition that was placed on the ballot by voters—a recommendation for a balanced budget. Essentially, the court said, "You can't use the initiative process," which is supposed to be guaranteed by the Constitution. This is an example of individuals who were trying to express themselves using the legal electoral process, but the system would not allow it. What would you do in a case like this?

A similar example can be seen in Proposition 24, which has to do with reducing the power of the state legislature. In particular, it reduces the power of certain key figures in the legislature who control the process, who control legislation that goes through. Implementation of Proposition 24, however, has been obstructed by the state legislature. Whether we agree or disagree with what the proposition contains, it was voted upon by the people of California and should be implemented.

Ideology and a certain outlook on life are at issue in this situation. The state supreme court is saying, "We know what is best for everybody; therefore, we are going to impose our view of what is right on the rest of society." That is something that voters have to be aware of. Any elected official who gives expression to that type of philosophy evidently feels that solutions come from a few somehow superior individuals. I don't see that as being a viable long-term solution. I think what we have to do is realize our own potential, solve our own problems, and help others to solve their problems.

By having a broad-based movement of that kind, which is essentially spiritual in nature, but manifested economically, politically, and so forth in the job market, you are going to have a broad-based change where people are made strong rather than weak. When you have strong individuals, they are able to help other people. Therefore, they cannot be victimized by the people who control the government, who play upon our weaknesses and our needs in order to manipulate us. If we feel strong and capable, we are certainly not going to say, "Okay, you govern our lives because we need you to make decisions for us." What I am getting at here is an entire outlook on life. We all know the problems that exist in America today. We have tremendous poverty, and we have tremendous problems across-the-board economically. We must decide whether we're going to solve those problems by having a handful of Americans somehow take care of them for us, or whether we're going to solve those problems by empowering ourselves.

During the 1984 Republican National Convention, President Reagan indicated in his address to some 11,000 mostly evangelical Christians that politics and religion needed to be partners. Is that what is meant by a spiritual approach?

Fundamentally, a spiritual approach means realizing that certain principles govern life, and if we follow those principles, we are going to prosper. We are going to benefit, and those around us will, also. Let's use the issue of inflation as an example. It is immoral to print money in order to make someone else's money worth less, just as it is immoral to engage in theft—or to rob someone or to lie or cheat or steal. We have to recognize that there are certain principles we need to apply in our own lives that will lead to prosperity, and those same principles, if they are good for an individual, are certainly good for society as a whole. They are universal principles that apply to all religions. President Reagan was speaking to a predominantly Christian audience because many of the people in this country, the majority of those who are actively religious, are Christian. But these principles are not limited to Christianity; they are universal.

Honesty, for example, is a principle that must be applied to the workings of government, just as it must be applied to our private lives. I find it fascinating that when we see certain powerful groups acting wrong, we seem to think that we need to give the government more power to control them. What we don't follow through to its logical conclusion is that these are the most powerful groups in our society, and in all likelihood, they are going to control the government that is implementing the new regulations and reforms. These groups can actually alter the reforms and regulations to their benefit. In 1916, income tax was brought forward as a tax on the rich; yet, the rich have loopholes and tax-free foundations. It is the average middle-class American who is burdened by a tremendous tax. The same thing happens in most areas of regulation. The airline, trucking, and railroad industries have opposed deregulation because they have used regulation in order to exclude competitors and keep prices high. We have to look to honesty to right such situations.

Honesty is the most fundamental principle. As individuals, we know we cannot get everything we want. We don't want to beg from other people. We want to be in a position of strength, where we are giving, not begging. And we don't want to be in a position where we are taking by force from someone else. That only leaves us with one option: Whenever we want something, we have to give somebody else what they want in return. This is fair and honest exchange. This is voluntary cooperation. Individuals' lives are generally based on voluntary cooperation—or they certainly should be. And there is no reason why our society should not follow the same principle. Honest exchange creates freedom. It creates freedom for oneself, and it allows other people freedom as well.

How does the Federal Reserve work, and is it working in our best interests? If not, how can we change it?

To understand how the Federal Reserve works, we have to look at its historical roots. We had a problem back in the 19th century where banks would simply print money, and then people would become aware that there were more bank notes circulating than there was gold to back those notes. So people would rush to the bank to get the gold out, and there would be a run on the bank. This would lead to collapse and a Depression. The people who put forward the idea of the Federal Reserve claimed that such an entity would end the business cycle of boom and bust. For that reason, Congress voted to create the Federal Reserve and gave it the power it currently enjoys. But if we look back over the past 70 years, we see that we've gone through two Depressions, eight or nine recessions, and the most prolonged period of inflation in our nation's history. The Federal Reserve hasn't worked, but the American people have not been aware enough of what's going on to put an end to the situation.

A lot of times, people consider the issue of gold as being something extreme, but if we look at the historical facts, gold has always been the workingman's protection against the government's power to inflate. If an individual could solve his problems by going into his basement and printing more money, many people would be tempted to do so. Governments are no different. A government solves its problem by going to its printing presses. The one hedge against this that the average person enjoys is an investment in gold or silver—or in the 1960s and 1970s, real estate.

What we can do as individuals to protect ourselves from the Fed's inflationary policies is invest in gold. But even more important, we can share information with each other. Once people realize what causes inflation—that it is an act of government policy, not an act of God—we can cut through all the nonsense and see who is supporting this kind of policy and why. We can exert political pressure for change, and political pressure does produce results. I think that is one thing we have seen over the past 20 years. When people become informed, educated, and active, government policies begin to change. It may be slower than we would desire, but it does take place.

In the 1960s, the price of gold was controlled by the government, and at that time, it was $36 an ounce. It was suggested that if the price was changed, mines would be opened up again in the gold rush country, and it would make a world of difference. Since then, the price of gold has skyrocketed; it's been up and down and back and forth again. Yet, we really don't see a whole lot of change, even though that price lid was lifted.

The reason we don't see a change is because we've allowed people to own gold. Back in the 1960s, it was illegal for Americans to own gold. In 1974, it became legal to own once again. The government stopped controlling the price of gold because it no longer *could* control it. In 1971, we went off the international gold standard because we'd printed so much money that the Europeans were rushing to redeem dollars for gold at $35 an ounce. We were going to run out of gold. We *had* to go off the gold standard. Although we've allowed gold to fluctuate, we have not gone back on a true gold standard, which would solve our nation's economic problems in that respect. What we need to see is an honest money system, and I use the word *honest* very intentionally.

If we went back on the gold standard, how would we possibly be able to keep all the banks in business, all of the money brokers in business? There is so much money out there that if we suddenly transferred to a gold standard, we wouldn't have enough gold to back it.

The purchasing power of gold would adjust to however much was in circulation. For example, there is no reason why a new car needs to cost $20,000. If there were less paper money, it could just as easily cost $6,000, and nobody would be any the worse for it. Similarly, it could cost 100 ounces of gold. There is no problem with that either. What you have to have is a situation that allows gold to find its own natural price in terms of what things are worth.

If gold became more valuable, if it had greater purchasing power, people would naturally go out and mine it, and that's what causes gold's purchasing power to remain stable over the years. If you look back 50 years, during the 1920s and 1930s, a $20 bill and a $20 gold coin were interchangeable. You could go into any clothing store and buy the finest suit in stock with either the gold coin or the $20 bill. Today, if you take an ounce of gold, you can still buy the nicest suit in town, but the $20 bill isn't even going to buy you the shirt or tie that they used to throw in free 50 years ago. The reason gold maintains its purchasing power is because if the price of gold becomes too high, it becomes worthwhile for somebody to mine it. But as soon as enough gold has been mined to keep up with the increase in productivity, it no longer becomes worthwhile to mine it, and so the price stabilizes there.

What you actually had during the 19th century when the United States was on the gold standard was a gradually declining price level because human creativity and productivity were increasing faster than the supply of gold. Therefore, prices were going down, and similarly, long-term interest rates were 3 and 4 percent. You could borrow money for 30 years and pay 3 percent interest, and I think we'd all like to go back to something like that.

There are millions of Americans giving financial advice today. Because the economy is so volatile, we all need this information to protect ourselves. Knowing how to earn more money and knowing how to invest our money is a matter of survival. In an honest society with a stable money system, it would not be worth anyone's while to speculate in the stock market, in the commodities market, or in bonds or gold because everything would have a stable value. If we were to go back on a gold standard, we would find that banks and many people involved in the financial business would begin doing something much more productive. I think that is something we would all benefit from.

As you pointed out in your book, banks are able to also create "funny" money. For every dollar they have on deposit, they can get eight more from the Federal Reserve. Wouldn't the banks be pretty upset about the idea of bringing back the gold standard because they would lose the ability to do that?

The reason we went off the gold standard in the first place was because of the banks. And the reason we've stayed off is because there have been enough people, in addition to banks, who benefit from inflation in the short run. In the long run, nobody benefits. And that is where you get back to spiritual principles. A banker may make millions of dollars a year on this type of manipulation. But he's benefiting at someone else's expense. In the long run, who's winning and who's losing? It's not the banker who's winning, because he's going to have to pay sooner or later, according to my vision of how life works and how the world works. So even in his long-term interests, it's best to get back into an honest, just system. From a practical point of view, that is why people have to be informed. That's why millions of Americans need to know how our system operates, so that we can exert political pressure. Unfortunately, those who benefit will not voluntarily relinquish their benefits.

In your view, the banker would suffer from taking advantage of others through the multimillion dollar manipulations because, in Hindu terminology, his karma would catch up with him. In Christian terminology, he would suffer in an afterlife. Basically, what you are including here is a spiritual life and applying it to economic reality.

In *The Prosperity Handbook*, I'm really interested in explaining what's going on in our economy and showing how we can build on fundamental principles that will create true prosperity—not only in our individual lives, but in our society as well. I don't view prosperity as just having a lot of money. That's nonsense. There are a lot of people with money who are poor emotionally and spiritually; they are even poor materially in the sense that they don't enjoy their wealth. In *The Prosperity Handbook,* I'm concerned with developing the full potential of each individual and realizing prosperity as an overall condition of life.

You mention in your book that the way to become prosperous is to do what you really love to do. A lot of people are in a situation where they don't feel that they can do what they really love to do because they feel trapped.

Many of us are in that position. If you look at statistics, there are only 5, 10, or 15 percent of the people in any generation who really know what they want to do and are doing it. And those are generally the people who are successful, the ones who are leading happy and prosperous lives. There must be something there we need to learn and apply in our own lives in order to get what we want out of life. One thing we have to recognize is that by discovering our own natural talents and abilities, we are going to be of the most service to others because we are going to be doing work that we enjoy. That's taking our own talents and expressing them, drawing them out with love, because when work is combined with love, something beautiful is produced. It is not only going to produce financial prosperity, it is going to produce a lot of happiness as well. We know the goal. The question is how do we get there.

In *The Prosperity Handbook,* we address that issue. First, we must set aside our preconceptions and boundaries. A lot of times, we think within ourselves and we are told by our environment—whether it's by family members, friends, or society as a whole—that we cannot do what we want to do. We don't have the education, we don't have the background, we don't have the support, we're never going to make it. We feel obligated to stay in that secure job. It's a tragedy because it is not necessary. People do not have to remain trapped.

The key to getting out of the boundaries is just setting them aside and being honest. We need to let go of our fears and listen to who we are inside. What is our inner voice saying? Each of us has dreams that we've had from birth and that come back periodically. A lot of times, we don't listen to that inner voice because it is too painful, and we are convinced that it's not real anyway. Or it can't become real. So it's easier to turn it off and turn on the television or something to drown it out rather than suffer by having unfulfilled ambitions. But we each need to ask ourselves, "What is it that I do well? What is it that other people tell me I am really good at? And what is it I enjoy?" In all probability, it is something that is one of our natural talents and abilities.

We have to keep in mind that we need to do something of value. Achieving happiness and satisfaction in life includes not only rest and play, but meaningful work as well. Once we have decided our key goal, our major goal in life, then it is time to get practical. We have to ask ourselves, "Well, where am I now? And where do I want to be? How am I going to get from here to there?" Maybe I'm a single parent, or maybe I have a wife and a family to support. Or maybe I've been in the same job for 20 years and changing careers would be a big transition. Wherever we are in our lives, we have to come up with a blueprint and systematically begin working toward the goal that we set for ourselves. And we are fortunate in America today. A hundred years ago, most people worked from sunup to sundown, six days a week. There were no options. There was no time to make a transition.

Today, we generally devote 40 hours a week to our jobs. And if we want to set aside some time, we can use it to begin working and moving in a new direction. But even if we know what we want and have begun working on a plan to achieve it, we still need to develop certain qualities in order to be successful. One such character quality, for example, is perseverance. I can have the greatest goal in the world. It can be very worthwhile for me to achieve it, but if I give up the first time I meet an obstacle, I'll never get there.

People grow, and remember, we are talking about a spiritual process here. We are talking about getting into the work that each of us is meant to be doing. We are talking about developing our God-given talents and abilities—or in different terminology, developing our Dharma. That's a spiritual path. We are going to grow most rapidly by being on that path and by serving others by being on it, but it's not necessarily going to be easy at first. And the reason it's not so easy is because it requires us to grow.

Perseverance is one character quality. Another is learning the value of cooperation. We have to learn the value of giving because we can't be successful in any "right" activity without performing that activity for the benefit of others.

You indicated earlier that all one needs to do is simply let go of the fears. That is difficult, especially considering that many of the fears are unconscious. One fear may be that "Even if I try to do what I want, I won't make it. I won't be good enough." That frequently is an unconscious fear. If one isn't even aware of that fear, how can it be dealt with?

Emerson said, "God does not implant within any human heart a desire which it does not also give the person the ability to fulfill." We are talking about a metaphysical concept here, and making the assumption that whatever desire we have within us is true and right. What we can always tell ourselves is, "Okay, there are problems. I'll deal with these problems. I'm not going to pretend they don't exist, but at least let me set the worries aside while I look at what I want to do. If I want to go back to my old job, I can always do that, too. Why not at least take the time to go within and look at myself? And let everything come up, because I'm not making any commitment by doing that. I'm just getting to know myself better." We could take that approach for starters. We don't have to pressure ourselves to make a final decision. We can just try to figure out who we are and what we really want. Once we begin to figure that out, we can begin to look at how practical a goal it is to achieve. This brings us back to that metaphysical concept of Emerson and all the great philosophers. Failure is giving up, and success is simply being persistent at driving toward a goal. If we persist, we are bound to get there sooner or later.

That's reminiscent of the story about Thomas Edison developing the lightbulb. Someone asked him, "How could you possibly have done 900 experiments trying to discover the electric lightbulb. How could you possibly persevere through 900 failures?" He replied, "What do you mean 'failed'? I learned 900 ways that the electric lightbulb would not work in order to arrive at the way it did." Sometimes it is a matter of how we see things.

There is a lesson in everything we encounter, and we have to have that attitude toward life. Years ago there were not many people earning a living writing books in this country. The figures are shocking. Not long ago, there were about 1,500 people whose sole occupation was writing books—out of a population of 230 million Americans. I'm one of those people. But I realized something, in terms of my own attitude, when somebody asked me what I thought about getting *The Prosperity Handbook* published. They were saying, "You know, a lot of times you've got to go through adversity before you achieve success." I thought, *Oh, my gosh, does that mean I'm not going to get this book published?* And then I looked back and saw how many times I'd been rejected by publishers in the past. It hadn't even dawned on me that I'd been rejected. What occurred to me was, "These people don't want the book? Okay, I'll go somewhere else." In the final analysis, we sold the book for a $1.3 million advance, and it was because we didn't give up (because we put into effect the principles that we describe in *The Prosperity Handbook*). I wasn't going to lay down and quit, because I had something that was of value, something that people needed. It was just a question of persisting and bringing it out to the people who need it and who see that need and can meet it.

You mentioned gold as a hedge against runaway inflation. What are some other recommendations?

It's important to diversify your savings when you understand what's going on in today's economy. On the one hand, the Fed can inflate the money supply and make our money worth less; in which case, we need gold to protect ourselves from that kind of inflation. On the other hand, there are 12 people in Washington who could decrease the supply of money and cause a Depression. And that has happened in the past—in our most recent Depression. There was a lot of unemployment, and it was all caused by the Federal Reserve's actions. If that were to take place again, you'd need money that was bearing interest. You'd want to have dollars that you could use to pay the mortgage or the rent and buy food. So, you want your money invested in a money market fund that is drawing interest and preferably one that invests in Treasury securities, because the reality is that our banking system in America today is very fragile, very vulnerable. You don't want to be in a situation where if there is a default by a Third World country, you are swept up in that crisis. In a money market fund that invests in Treasury securities, you're going to be able to get your money out. That's also a reason for investing a portion of your savings in gold; if there were that type of crisis, the government, in all probability, would print money to bail the banks out, and you'd have even more rapid inflation.

Another thing that offers protection from inflation is owning real estate. Real estate prices are very high today. Interest rates are high. That means mortgages are high. It is difficult to buy and sell land. It's certainly not as easy as it was in the 1950s and 1960s. But if we are going to be located in one place over the long term, it is still a good idea to own property. We have to be careful that we don't get in over our heads. If we're making payments on a mortgage and we lose our job, we don't want to go bankrupt and be left with nothing. That's the last thing I'd want to see happen to anyone.

Those are really the three fundamentals: gold, a money market fund drawing interest, and real estate. When you start talking about other things, such as stocks, you are getting into the speculative realm. The advice that we give in *The Prosperity Handbook* is designed for safety rather than speculation. If you are in a situation where values are constantly fluctuating, as they were in the 1980s, you don't want to be in a situation where you are losing value.

A money market fund is basically making money on the manipulation of money. That's how money market funds generate their money. What are the spiritual aspects of that?

In the investment section of *The Prosperity Handbook,* there are several chapters devoted to changing yourself, developing yourself, and realizing your goals. It doesn't necessarily require a large investment, but it is the most important kind of investment you can make because you are investing in yourself to produce more wealth in the future. Similarly, it is very desirable to invest in productive enterprises. Unfortunately, our society penalizes productivity and rewards speculation. We have to recognize that. Ideally, we'd like to live in a society where money that is saved is invested in companies that produce new technology, such as solar or organic farming technology. And it is still something that we can do with some of our savings. But we also have to recognize that people who put all of their money on the line are sitting targets for those people in our society who will manipulate things in order to make other people's money worth less. As a matter of self-protection, until we get back to a society where productivity and honesty are rewarded, we've got to preserve the purchasing power of our money rather than simply acting out of principle and making ourselves vulnerable.

The same is true of gold. You could say that gold's not producing interest. It's not really producing anything other than insurance—peace of mind. Our economy needs to get back to a gold standard where any money you have is nothing but gold, essentially, unless you are invested in a company. In that case, you just have a stable monetary unit. When you had your money invested in the bank and it was gold there in the bank, the bank would research the companies to invest in and would invest that money to produce a greater profit in the future.

I know a number of people who are money investment managers. The people I know are generally successful. But, when you look at the figures, most people who are investing other people's money, after inflation and taxes, are losing money—if not year after year, then certainly in off-years. These are people who have nothing to do, who have no career other than studying the markets and investing, and they are losing money. When I look at the implications of that for the average person who does not have the time and energy to go to a company and investigate the situation, I see that the average person is really vulnerable. That is the person liable to be the one who provides profits for the other speculators, the ones who are in it full time.

I think that the real, long-term solution requires applying these principles to our own lives in terms of investing in ourselves and investing in a business that is going to be productive and is going to be of true value to society. We can channel money there, recognizing at the same time our limitations, and not throwing our money out just out of good intentions. We can protect ourselves and work on a social level to change the system that is causing us to take these self-protective steps. I'm convinced that we are going to return to a society where savings and productivity are rewarded rather than penalized. And we really need to solve the problem on that level.

When I give tax advice, I can talk about a way to cut taxes, but the best way to cut taxes is to cut the size of government and to cut the IRS. While we can gain knowledge, and I can put forth knowledge in *The Prosperity Handbook* that will allow us to protect ourselves financially, that doesn't satisfy me. I am not content to get in a little rowboat and float off by myself while the whole ship goes down. I think the only situation that I'm going to be satisfied with is if enough Americans have the knowledge to protect themselves and can implement that knowledge and bring it to government so that the whole country can prosper in the years ahead. What I find most inspiring is that by applying these principles in our own lives, we automatically are doing a tremendous amount to change government, because we are part of the solution rather than the problem.

By following the advice in *The Prosperity Handbook*, people can begin to change their own lives, and if the knowledge becomes widespread, it will no longer be possible for the power blocks to continue imposing their agenda on America. It will no longer be possible for inflation to continue, for the business cycle to continue. Productive businesses will no longer be penalized, and new technologies will be developed because big corporations will no longer be allowed to squash them.

What exactly can people do to effect change relative to taxes?

The best thing to do relative to taxes is to work at the governmental level to cut the bite that the government is taking out of our paychecks. That's the most effective thing we can do now.

One way to try to implement such changes is to write your congressman. There are some people who refuse to pay taxes, and I don't condemn anybody who doesn't pay taxes, but I don't advocate that method either. Certainly, you legally avoid as many taxes as you can.

We have to let the people in government know that we want change. In the situation previously described, where the California Supreme Court turned down the balanced budget amendment, we were basically being told that it is not the right of the people of California to tell their legislature what to do. That is an outrage. We had one of the most sensible proposals that has come down the road in years to control government spending. It simply instructed the government not to spend any more than it was bringing in, and it was voted down by the state supreme court. The state legislature wasn't any better. It could have passed that kind of resolution if it had wanted to, but it was the people of California who demanded it. We have to bring about change by letting those in government know that if they continue in their obstructionist path, they are going to be removed.

There are obstacles standing between the American people and prosperity—between ourselves and a society that is based on honesty and integrity in government. A lot of times people ask me, "Well, what you are talking about? Is it very realistic?" And I say, "You know, I go to Washington all the time and meet with a lot of people on Capitol Hill, and believe me, there are a lot of people there who care more about their jobs than care about doing what's right." But does that mean we should give up trying to promote honesty and integrity in government? It doesn't. I'd like to think of *The Prosperity Handbook* as a tool. Without knowledge, there is nothing we can do. If we do not know what the problem is, we are not going to be able to propose solutions. So I view it as a tool—not only for self-protection, but also to bring about social change.

To continue with the question of tax avoidance, isn't it true that tax avoidance is only available to those who have money? As you pointed out earlier, it is the middle class who pays the taxes. Tax shelters are not available to people with ordinary middle-class incomes. You need large discretionary amounts of money to be able to exercise tax shelter benefits and advantages. How do we change this?

The average person who is on a salary is in an especially bad position, because wage earners do not have the deductions that someone who is self-employed has. Their money is just siphoned off every other week or every month. However, if you study taxes, there are things you can do. You can start a business on the side. Again, you have to have the objective of making money with that business. You can research it in order to take what steps you can to cut down the tax load. But the thing is, the special-interest groups know that they can place a big burden on the back of the American taxpayer, and there is not much that the average worker can do to get out of it because of the people who are benefiting.

Just to give you an example: The American taxpayer is subsidizing the big banks in this country, which have loaned hundreds of millions of dollars to the Third World. Those governments cannot repay the money. The banks don't want to write it off as a loss, so they get Congress to give taxpayer money to the International Monetary Fund to give to the governments of Brazil and Mexico. This money, in turn, is given to the banks; therefore, we are essentially paying for the bank's losses. We have a situation where the bank makes a profit on a loan, and the profit goes to the bank. But when the bank has a loss, it is the taxpayer who gets the bill. You see that across-the-board in America today.

There is so much money to be made from taxing the American worker that as individuals it is hard for us to escape that. If individuals could escape it easily, everyone would be escaping it, and we wouldn't be serving any longer as beasts of burden for those who benefit. What we have to recognize is that we can't solve the problem on an individual basis. The solution comes when as a group we realize the predicament that we are in and demand an end to that kind of special-interest legislation. If the government was not spending money on that kind of program to bail out the banks, if the government was not giving money to large corporations, if the government was not paying $20 billion a year to farmers for not growing crops, and if the government was not subsidizing tobacco farming at the same time as paying for cancer research, our taxes would go way down because there wouldn't be anything to spend them on.

The Grace Commission report showed that $424 billion could be cut over three years without any problem. The question was not what new programs should be cut, but rather, what fat can be cut out of existing programs without questioning their purposes. One example of the difficulty involved in cutting spending can be seen in military base closings. Military bases that even the Pentagon wants to get rid of are kept because they supply jobs to a local area and the congressman makes alliances.

However, if there is widespread understanding of how our economy works, we can bring about change. I'm optimistic about the country because I think there is a spiritual revolution going on in America today. I think more and more people are realizing that happiness does not just come from material things.

The problems that we are experiencing are created by people focusing on material issues rather than spiritual ones, and by people thinking that if there are only a limited amount of resources, they'd better take what they can from other people. This is a narrow, short-sighted view of life, and stems from thinking that this is the only life there is and we'd better make the most of it.

In opposition to that, I think there are a growing number of people in this country who have an entirely different view of life. Their view suggests that there is nothing wrong with prosperity, with enjoying material goods, that there is nothing wrong with having a good life physically and materially. But it's not worth violating spiritual laws in order to do so, because real happiness is based on following these spiritual laws and growing spiritually. The purpose of life, in this case, is to know and serve God. And when you are talking about fulfillment coming from the knowledge of God, then we can no longer accept the idea of manipulating other people for material benefit.

For whatever reason, there are an expanding number of people in this country and throughout the world who are turning to spiritual solutions for material problems. There is rightness to this. Nobody can justify a government program that victimizes the elderly. Nobody can justify a government program that pays people for not growing crops when you have people around the world who are starving. As this attitude becomes more widespread and we realize our power, we realize that we are the majority. If we inform ourselves about what's going on in our economy, in our government, and know what we can do to solve those problems and share this knowledge, we are going to make our power known, and it is going to be expressed in society.

⁂

EPILOGUE

Here is still another view of the money scene, which addresses monetary and political institutions and policies. Taylor speaks of the gold standard, the Federal Reserve, the IRS, and more, but all the while, he makes the connection to the spiritual. He also emphasizes the importance of inner work as the method to clarify our actions around money. At the same time, he points to economic realities that most of us need to see more clearly, such as how the global economy affects the taxpayer negatively. Both the practical and the profound are part of Taylor's message. Our personal actions around money need to be guided and informed by the spiritual, rather than the material, according to him. As we place more emphasis on spiritual principles and act from our deeper self, then our attitudes and experience of money will be transformed as well.

CHAPTER FIVE

True Wealth

Paul Hwoschinsky and Michael Toms

PROLOGUE

In the strange and volatile economic territory that we inhabit, it is difficult to penetrate the dense fog separating the economists and so-called economic experts from the rest of us. Money and wealth are clearly among the great mysteries for most of us. More often than not, we equate money with wealth. True wealth may indeed include a great deal more than just financial resources. Money may be only a means to another end. So the challenge rests in earning money to live life, rather than living to earn money. Paul Hwoschinsky explores the issues of money and wealth in his book, True Wealth. *Paul was a venture capitalist for 20 years. He is also an avid backpacker and wilderness photographer. His work has taken him to the Sierra Nevada; the Alps; and to the mountains of Alaska, Peru, Nepal, Tibet, Bhutan, and Ladakh. Currently, he is involved in helping to create microlending projects in various Himalayan communities.*

⁂

***MICHAEL TOMS**: It would seem that the idea for your book and your understanding of true wealth came about because of your trips to the mountains. How did your travels help you understand money and wealth?*

PAUL HWOSCHINSKY: In the early 1980s, when I was in Nepal in the Himalayas, I had a most remarkable experience. I was in the Annapurna sanctuary up at about 19,000 feet, surrounded by the great peaks of the Himalaya and Annapurna Mountains. It's like standing in the bottom of a salad bowl, with clouds drifting in and out. When the sun goes down, everything turns chalk white. I had just finished photographing this remarkable place, when my lead sirdar, a Buddhist Sherpa, came up to me. He said, "Paul, may I ask you a personal question?" I'd been climbing with this man for a full month; there was a great deal of trust between us. I said, "Certainly." Then, he asked me if I was rich—which absolutely took me by surprise. I just looked at him, because I didn't know how to answer. After all, my airfare was ten times his annual salary. But then suddenly I realized what the answer was. And I said, "Fhu, I'm not terribly rich, but I'm quite wealthy." Then it was his turn to be surprised. That night in our tents, at minus 30 degrees Fahrenheit, the two of us talked a lot about the differences between wealth and riches.

About two months later, back in the United States, four or five people asked me to do a workshop on money. They thought I knew about money since I was a venture capitalist. And I said, "You know, money for me is like electricity. I use it, but I don't understand it. I don't feel competent to do a workshop on money, but I will do one on wealth." And that's how it started. One of the things that happened was that I really began to question what constituted wealth. The Sherpa, who didn't have many riches, seemed to me to be tremendously wealthy. He knew who he was, and he was in touch with his own human spirit and soul. He had an incredibly wonderful place to live—no traffic jams. He had very close and fulfilling relationships. And when I reconsidered my answer to his question, I began to wonder if I had answered correctly. Was I, in fact, wealthy? And that's how the concept began, and later it blossomed into the book *True Wealth.*

I learned more as I began to develop the seminars. I discovered in my research that wealthy people seemed to focus more on *being* than *having*—although *having* wasn't an impediment to wealth. People who were wealthy seemed to connect who they were with what they did. The other surprising discovery I made was that financial assets are basically not financially driven. When you realize that experientially in your life, more options than ever show up. It becomes very exciting.

When you say that financial assets are not financially driven, what do you mean?

Let me give an example of how this works. A friend who had been fired came to me. He'd been the officer of a company, and he was pretty dejected. He asked, "What shall I do? Who wants to hire an officer who's been fired?" I said, "Probably lots of people. "Let's take a look at your nonfinancial balance sheet." As part of my inquiry into values and wealth, I also had to look at nonfinancial resources. He wanted to know what was in a nonfinancial balance sheet. I asked, "Well, what might be there?" He drew a complete blank. I began asking him questions to help him list his nonfinancial assets.

I asked him about his education—he had a Ph.D. I asked him about his health—he was a smoker, overweight, and didn't exercise. Then I asked about his relationship with his wife, with their children, and with his children from a former marriage. I told him that I didn't need the answers, but he did. Then I told him to list some really close friends. He said, "You know, I don't have any really close friends. So I said, "Well, you rang my doorbell. Let's take a look at what I can offer." I began to make a matrix of all the people I knew and the contacts I had, which surprised even me. This elicited a name from him, and we began to find out who that person was. After about four or five names, we could see the tremendous wealth that was available to him.

To make a long story short, he is now a consultant in his very narrow specialty of physics and is doing very well. He now makes a six-figure annual income because he was able to convert a non-financial resource into a financial one. On the other hand, Steve DeVore, who started Sybervision, managed to take a nonfinancial liability—in his case, polio—and turn it into a business, which is another wonderful story. What really came to me is that we separate money from the rest of our lives, when in actual fact, we need to join all those assets.

You are suggesting that wealth is a great deal more than just the money we have in the bank. You mentioned relationships and health. What other kinds of nonfinancial assets do we have?

Different people have different assets. Bob Hope, for example, used his ability to be humorous and built a whole business around it. His humor and creativity were certainly nonfinancial assets. And Steve DeVore, whom I already mentioned, started Sybervision, which is an extraordinary company. He had polio at age two and couldn't walk. His doctors wanted to cut all the tendons in his legs so that he'd look more presentable in a wheelchair. But his mother wouldn't agree to that. Instead, each afternoon she took him to the park, and she'd say, "Now Steve, watch that person walk; watch that person run." Pretty soon, he got over his polio and became an athlete. When it came time to finish college and earn a living, he went back to his mother and asked her what had really happened. She told him as much as she knew—that it was a kind of programming. So he formed Sybervision, a company that creates tapes to help people realize their full potential. He turned a nonfinancial liability into a thriving business.

One of our workshops was attended by an interesting young woman who had a bad back. When she was doing her nonfinancial balance sheet, she showed her bad back as an asset. That was novel to me. She explained that if it hadn't been for her bad back, she wouldn't have become attentive to diet, yoga, meditation, and exercise. All of those things helped her get over the bad back and achieve really great health.

What I suddenly realized was that most of our resources are nonfinancial, but we ignore them or don't really see the power in them. Of course, this is a difficult time right now. It's a time when people need to take a look at all of their resources and bring them to bear on who they are and what they do as a way of being causal about their lives.

In True Wealth, *you describe a number of exercises—one of which is writing your own obituary. What is the value of that exercise?*

When I wrote my own obituary, I cried for half an hour. It was a very moving experience. Writing your own obituary is a long-standing exercise, but it was meaningful to me in the context of *True Wealth* because it requires people to reflect on their lives. I didn't want the obituary just to say that Paul Hwoschinsky was a venture capitalist, he made this deal and that deal, and was survived by relatives. What I wanted was a description of the essence of Paul. Perhaps the following example will clarify what I mean.

One person wrote: "He was held back mostly by fears of taking full responsibility for doing what he wanted. He blamed others for his lack of courage. He never learned to relax. He never found peace but enjoyed the trip. He had a hard time accepting his deficiencies and pushed to change them, but he could reconcile all the paradoxes with laughter. Maverick, mystic, artist, fire walker, passionate traveler, cowboy, therapist, builder, lover. He was someone who created a clear means for people to become extraordinary."

That doesn't give the person's occupation; and it doesn't reveal age, marital status, hobbies, or net worth, but you have a sense of his person and his being. And through that exercise, he was able to get in touch with his inner self. It's an exercise that is very difficult for a lot of people and was certainly difficult for me as well.

One of the discoveries we make through this exercise is that when we get in touch with who we are and connect that with what we do, we experience a sense of rightness and power that leads to creativity. For example, I get wonderfully focused and also excited when I'm in the field photographing. I become super alive and suffused with creativity. When I get a creative idea in my business work or in my relationships, the same thing happens. I can actually feel it physically, so I know I'm in touch with it. I know that quality is important to me, and I want the exercise to help people get in touch with their own unique qualities.

Just because people are in the same field, they don't necessarily experience things or express themselves in the same way. For example, Martin Luther King was a humanitarian, a man of peace. Armand Hammer was also a humanitarian. But the two illustrate interesting personal differences. One traveled around in his private 727; the other one had a private car, and that was about it. They are both dead now. One left a huge estate; the other, a very small one. But they were both tied to the same sense of service and peace and humanitarianism. Each of them managed to connect who they were to what they did; and their legacies, though similar in intent, bear the individual stamp of each of their personalities.

How would you explain someone like Howard Hughes and the way he ended his days? Here was a man of immense wealth, riches, and financial assets, yet his life seemed to be one of despair.

I think we all see people who are extremely alive. And some of them have lots of wealth, and some of them don't have any wealth but lots of riches. It's interesting to note the differences. Riches don't *seem* to matter—but they *do* matter. That's the dance. That's the curious polarity. We learn more about health in the context of illness. We learn more about life and breath in the context of death and dying. So it's important, I think, to just get into the place where we know who we are.

Does it follow that we learn more about money by being poor?

There is nothing wrong with having money or not having money. That's not the issue at all. Wealth is derived from an early word that means "well-being." And what we are about is creating well-being. There is a chapter in *True Wealth* on resources in which I simply ask people to make a list of their financial and nonfinancial riches and wealth in order to bring them to bear on their vision of life and their purpose.

I define vision as being an expression of who we are, and purpose is really an expression of what we do. Goals simply represent how we go about doing what we do. And in terms of who we are, I think we all represent certain qualities in our lives. Some examples of those qualities include beauty, brotherhood, compassion, courage, creativity, energy, enthusiasm, freedom, faith, patience, service, and serenity. Let's take, for example, someone who says,

"I represent the quality of beauty. Now what should I do with my life?" In actual fact, that person could be an artist and *show* beauty—through sculpture, painting, music, writing, or dance. Knowing the experiential connection between the form we choose and the quality it represents is what brings a sense of rightness to our living. As I work with people in workshops and also experience it in my own life, that's the piece that is absolutely vital—seeing that connection.

Artists in any phase of the arts don't necessarily make a lot of money simply because of their particular profession. These are people who have made that experiential connection. So what makes the jump from the connection to one's vision and being able to generate financial resources?

Many people may choose not to have financial resources. Mother Teresa is one of them. That's her choice. She is someone who expresses love in her life, and she doesn't need to create personal riches with it. On the other hand, she generates a lot of financial resources to support her mission, so in that sense she is generating wealth. She does that by following what Joseph Campbell calls her "bliss." But she's also causal, and that really is where I think a lot of people fall down.

We do have to take responsibility for making our lives work for us. But if we are clear about who we are, clear about what we want to do, and we bring our financial and nonfinancial resources together, it's extraordinary what can happen. When I was looking for a publisher—and I am not in the publishing business, I'm not a full-time author—I had to struggle. It took probably two and a half years to find a publisher. So I went to my nonfinancial balance sheet and practiced what I preached. I finally found my path to Ten Speed Press and George Young, who said, "Where have you been?

I've been looking for this manuscript for five years." So it can happen, and it does happen.

During these difficult times, I think we need to look at our resources. There are so many examples of people who have been Ph.D.'s in one field, and who totally changed jobs and are working in other fields now, or are starting up little companies and doing things that are really more in tune with who they are. And we have, especially in our country, tremendous wealth in our education and our experiences. We need to do some of these exercises and really honor our total resources. When we do, magical things happen. New options occur. When we begin to experience that financial assets are often nonfinancially driven, we begin to see new options.

It's a very exciting thing. When people start to work with the nonfinancial balance sheet, they surprise themselves. And the important thing is to illuminate the nonfinancial liabilities that block the assets because then we can do something about them. If they are not highlighted, then we can't. What we're really striving for is to create a deep awareness, and from that, gain empowerment in our lives. That's really what it is. It's being causal. And that's the great thing that needs to be learned now in the Soviet Union and Eastern Europe and places where people have not had freedoms. We have the freedom to do those things.

Then the question becomes, "How do I feed myself with nonfinancial assets? How do I pay the rent?"

Even though we may tie in with the qualities of beauty and freedom, we still get stuck on freeways, still need to pay bills, and all the rest of it. But when we take a look at all of our resources and are confirmed in the thing we want to do, there is a richness and a wealth that comes from doing that which is really part of us and who we are. It sustains us and offers the creativity to make the other work. We can't just do what we've always wanted to do for one reason or another and trust that someone will come along and pay us. But if we connect with a quality and start to be causal about it, it is amazing the roots we will find.

How do you define causal*?*

Being causal means that we can rely on ourselves to find our way along many paths. We get stopped because we tend to think we don't have resources, when we really do. For example, people don't honor the fact that they are healthy. They don't honor the fact that they have an education. They don't honor the fact that they have friends. But when we start to look at our friends and start to explore all those contacts, it is amazing where we can go. It's real wealth.

In terms of finding jobs, what I've always done is started a company and hired myself. I was the first employee. I've done that several times, and it's highly entrepreneurial. We need to find out where we are relative to being comfortable with risk taking. That's part of it. To that end, I've developed a kind of matrix, which is very systemic. I ask people to deal with vision and purpose, and from that, to develop financial and nonfinancial goals that are very specific. Next, they need to bring their resources to bear—both financial and nonfinancial—and look at their financial and nonfinancial tolerance for risk. Once we've done all that, we can address all the possibilities that are available. That entails looking at our life as a whole system. And that's why it's very psychosynthetically driven; that is to say, there is a principle in nature where individual segments come together to form greater wholes.

What is the connection between risk taking and wealth?

First of all, it's okay to be a risk taker, and it's okay not to be a risk taker. Each of us must decide for ourselves which type of person we are. Fear is generally part of this whole thing. In fact, the financial markets are driven by greed and fear. When people act out of fear, the market is affected by fear.

In our own investment practices, I think we can all go back in our mind's eye and find times when we acted probably out of a little bit of greed and other times when we acted out of a little bit of fear. What I propose is that we base our actions on our personal vision and purpose. When we can operate in that context—whether we're risk takers or not—we're on target. We also need to be clear on what the risk is—what it involves. We all know that financial risk tends to be buying stocks, bonds, commodities, or whatever. But it's the nonfinancial area where people take risks and don't realize it. Probably the greatest nonfinancial risk that most of us take is in choosing a spouse—people don't think twice about it. But the risk is great, and one of the consequences is a failed marriage—divorce.

There are innumerable other nonfinancial risks we take as well. Choosing to have children is a risk; changing careers is a risk. Telling an employer that his policy is good or not good is a risk. Smoking, drinking, overeating, or otherwise misusing our bodies is a tremendous risk. Facing or not facing our own death is another nonfinancial risk. Physically rescuing another person is a risk, and there are many stories of people who have done that. There are many nonfinancial risks that we all take every day. Some risks are very conscious choices, while others, such as choosing a partner, are not really recognized as risks at all. If we really look at ourselves, we realize, to one degree or another, that we are all risk takers. And we don't really honor it. I'd like people to look at their lives and say, "I know I can take those risks. I can do that." Or, "I'm uncomfortable with that, and I won't do that." It's okay to say that, too. It's not a judgment issue.

It is a matter of taking a look at the environment in which we live, looking at those forces over which we have no control but with which we need to reckon in order to succeed, and pressing on with the resources that we have or can acquire relative to our vision and purpose. That's really the issue. And that's what I mean by being causal. When we take a look at that, we are really developing a life plan, but we are doing it within a system that is integrated. It requires bringing individual segments together to create a new whole. And what I am asking people to do is to create that new whole.

You indicate that connections and relationships with others are part of our nonfinancial resources. What about experts? Are people who can tell us what to do with our money nonfinancial resources?

Advisors and experts are available both financially and nonfinancially, and I ask people to decide whether they want to use advisors or not. Using a financial advisor is common, but there are also a lot of nonfinancial advisors available to us. Friends, counselors, clergymen, and rabbis, for example, are people who can advise us. What we need to remember is that we are responsible for what we teach, and we are equally responsible for what we are taught. When we consult an advisor to help us with our life plan, we need to realize that we are responsible for what is being taught. That is to say, if a stockbroker advises us to buy particular stocks and they go down, even though we followed that person's advice, we can't blame that person. Ultimately, we have to rely on ourselves to evaluate advice we receive, and say, "Okay, in my judgment, I will use that advice."

Most people aren't really aware of the fact that we all are responsible for what we are taught, but it's an important concept to understand. And it seems as though, when we deal with economies, they are above us and out of our control. There is something frightening about the economy. We have to understand that the economy is just an expression of all of us acting separately but simultaneously. An economist is simply someone who watches that process and comments on it. We are all a part of that environment. We all are a part of making the market go up and down.

In the 1980s, for example, we built a tremendous amount of debt. As a nation, we created more debt in eight years than we did in the preceding 200 years. Corporately, with leveraged buyouts, we created so much debt that finally it tumbled down. As individuals, we created a tremendous amount of credit card debt. We were responsible for all of what happened. I mean, we voted—we elected all the people in the Congress. We elected the president. We were all acting separately but together.

I remember the story of a friend of mine who had an apartment for rent, and a couple came to apply. He turned them down. They had two jobs, but they had 14 credit cards—$36,000 worth of credit card debt. He was afraid that if one of those jobs fell through, he would have to evict them. So there again, they did something of their own free will and created that situation. I just want people to be conscious of the fact that they are a part of creating all of that.

In 1987, when I was in Nepal, the stock market crash occurred. It was an interesting experience. A friend of mine had gotten hurt on one of our climbs. I went down to check up on him with one of the U.S. doctors. The doctor came out of the hut and asked if we had heard about the Dow. And I said, do we spell it *Dow* or *Tao*? And he said, "Well, the Dow fell 508 points last week." And I said, "Well I'm here for Tao, not Dow."

What had happened was that some of us had seen the tremendous boom that was happening in that stock market, so we sold all of our stocks before the crash came. I had no idea it would come so soon, but it came. We can't always know all those things for sure, but we can create an awareness—and that includes a nonfinancial awareness—of what's happening. We need to relate that awareness to who we are and what we do. Then things tend to work. And if we are in the soup, that's okay. We can begin to find our way out of that condition by asking ourselves who we are, what we like to do, what the environment is like, what advisors are available to us, and where we are going.

There is an entire section in *True Wealth* that deals with the environment—the nonfinancial as well as the financial environment. All of this is really a matter of being aware of who we are and what's around us so that we can react causally. So much of this we take for granted and don't really think about.

What's an example of a nonfinancial environment?

Being a smoker, for example, creates a certain kind of environment. Companies can create environments that are not really safe with regard to health. There are many conditions. We can be in a physical environment or in a relationship that isn't healthy. People need to look at all their assets and liabilities. Usually the outcome is that we begin to ask questions: Are my relationships what they might be, what they could be? How can I make them better? When we start to ask those questions and illuminate some of those liabilities, we begin to grow. And then those relationships—if they are close and if they are strong—are tremendous sources of hope and courage.

What about investment in very chaotic times? What do we do about where we place our money and our financial resources?

I think we do whatever we need to do in the context of *who* we are and *where* we are in our lives. We need to ask ourselves how much of a risk we want to take, what is sensible relative to our goals, which flow from who we are and what we do. I can see a scenario where some people might take some pretty big risks. A newly married couple, for example, might have pretty good jobs, no liabilities, and no children. This couple may see an advisor who tells them of an opportunity in a given area. So, they may sell short, go into commodities, or start their own business. They are in a position to take risks at this point in their lives. When Steve Jobs formed Apple Computer, he really bet on his total person, his vision of what might be, and so he put everything on the line. He took a tremendous risk in starting his own company and ended up founding one of the great computer companies of the world.

On the other hand, people near or in retirement are probably not going to take the financial risks that younger people would take. It depends on where we are in life. Certainly, there are older people who love risk taking. They love the excitement, and they have skills in a given area—in real estate, for example—so they have an intuitive sense about risk taking. But whatever we do, we have to do it in the context of who we are. And remember, goals are simply a discussion of how we are going to go about doing what we do, and they are divided into financial and nonfinancial segments. We have to be sure that we have nonfinancial goals.

Many people are conditioned by the false myth that to make a million dollars, all they've got to do is find the right thing. Many people lose a lot of money that way.

They do, and they really don't make an inquiry into what that environment is all about. They don't talk to people who are in the business and find out what their experiences have been. They don't talk to people who have lost and find out why they lost. It's very important to take responsibility for what we do. We must all understand and be responsible for what we are taught as well as what we teach. When we start to do that, we realize that we have the capability to think things through. That's how we begin developing a life plan.

You seem to be indicating that most of us have been co-dependent with money. And with wealth in general we depend on someone else to handle it all—the bank, a lawyer, or a stockbroker. We really don't look at the whole picture.

It's okay to turn money over to a broker; that isn't the problem. The problem lies in not looking at that broker and deciding that's the way to do it at this time. Nature reaches for wholeness. And when we have recessions, it's just nature looking to self-correct. And it will. What happens is that the debt gets wiped out. People go through bankruptcy, and we start again. That's healing. So we need to not be fearful of that but to understand that there are natural cycles that we all go through. And since the economy's really built up by each of us acting separately but together, it's a very healing, human, dynamic thing.

Why do you think so many people have such an emotional charge around money?

In this country, we equate money with success and power, and some people have been able to build extraordinary riches through the democratic free market system. It's just been extraordinary. So others look at that and say, "Gosh, I want that, too." But we have to be able to keep focused on what is really important.

I know from experience that thoughts of our own mortality can sharpen our focus quickly. One day I woke up and urinated blood. I looked in the mirror and thought, *Okay, it's cancer. I'd better go see a doctor, and I suppose there won't be a whole lot of time left.* Then, I began thinking about all the values I held and all the things that I really wanted to do. Had I said all the things that I needed to say to my wife? To my children? To my friends? To my enemies? And then I thought, *Hey, you silly fool, why don't you call the doctor?* So I called the doctor, and he laughed at me and said, "Look, Paul, when you had a physical yesterday, I checked to see if your prostate was large or small, and in the process, I may have ruptured some blood vessels. That's probably all it is. Call me in the morning if it persists." And I had my life back again.

But from that experience, I quickly got in touch with what was truly important. And in crisis that's what happens to us. When we go through a divorce, when we lose our jobs, when we have a recession, when we have a depression, that's what is real. And my sense is that we create our own crisis in order to realize and become who we already are.

I have several friends who have cancer, and they are going through this same process of thinking and questioning. But we can also simulate this experience, using the obituary exercise. That's what I would like people to do. It helps them focus on important questions: Who are they? Do they represent freedom, peace, compassion, love? And when they find out, how can they integrate that in their lives to bring a sense of rightness and at the same time be able to pay bills, get stuck in traffic, and do all the things that we all have to do on a daily basis?

What about the future? None of us can predict the future, but you are suggesting—and a lot of other people are as well—that we are in for some hard times. What do you see those hard times actually looking like?

In financial terms, this particular recession or depression or whatever we want to call it is debt driven. This is the first time that's been true. Earlier depressions have been inventory driven. So the resolution of this one is to get the debt down. And that's going to happen in a lot of ways. A lot of companies are going to go bust. There will be a lot of mergers. There's going to be a lot of dislocation as merging companies let employees go and other companies take them on. Some industries are going to disappear. Some industries are going to come into play. And so we'll create more jobs in the end than we ever realized. It will work out, but it will mean some dislocation in the meantime.

If we take a look at our financial balance sheet and truly look at it as USA, Inc., we see the value in the great granaries of the Midwest, the productive capabilities in our factories, and the innovation of our people. One thing economists tend not to do is take into account the causality or innovation or creativity of people when they are in a pinch. And we are very creative. A lot of things are going to be built out of nothing. And that's exciting. I tend to have hope for all of us, myself included. I may lose everything that I have because of some chaotic event, but in the process, if I'm really satisfied that I'm realizing who I am, then there's always that sense of rightness. And at whatever age, I'm just going to have the energy to see that through. I want all of us to do that, and I hope *True Wealth* will help people integrate all those pieces of themselves so they create a greater whole.

There are some older cultural examples of all debts being forgiven. Imagine it's a Jewish Jubilee year, and all debts are forgiven.

In a sense, that's what bankruptcy is. And there will be people who will go through that. In the *Wall Street Journal* just the other day, there was an example of a couple who were up to $30,000 or

$40,000 in credit card debt. And their reaction was, "We never thought we'd have to pay it back. That was their reaction. They created their own crisis, and they will learn from that. And they will come out of that either a whole lot stronger, or they will really go to the bottom. It's up to them. We all react the way we react. I'm just asking people to find out who they are. Problems in our financial realities are also opportunities for us to grow.

❋ ❋ ❋

EPILOGUE

Former venture capitalist and entrepreneur Hwoschinsky reminds us that financial assets are often nonfinancially driven and that true wealth has more to do with experiencing than having. The first step is to become fully aware of who one is. We then learn to combine who we are with what we do and gain power over both our financial and nonfinancial resources. He shows us how our nonfinancial assets and resources can create financial ones. To experience true wealth has more to do with knowledge and attitude than with something beyond our control. According to Hwoschinsky, investing is a process of making appropriate choices. We do this best when we have a clear view of who we are and where we want to go. There is a profound connection between living our dream and manifesting true wealth.

Money is only one part of a total system that produces wellbeing. Earning money needs to relate to living life fully rather than living to earn money.

❋ ❋ ❋ ❋ ❋ ❋

CHAPTER SIX

The Experience of Prosperity

Shakti Gawain and Michael Toms

PROLOGUE

Most people equate prosperity with money. If only they had more of it, they would prosper. In point of fact, happiness, fulfillment, and real prosperity have little or nothing to do with how much money and how many material things we might possess. Rather, real prosperity has more to do with living a meaningful life and experiencing joy and fulfillment in meeting our hearts' and souls' longings. One of those who has spent the past two decades showing us how we can have more prosperity in our lives at all levels is Shakti Gawain. She is recognized as a leader in the world-consciousness movement. A publisher and author of ten books, she's taught workshops around the world. Her bestselling classic, Creative Visualization, *has sold over 2.5 million copies in English and has been translated into 30 editions worldwide. She's also the author of* Living in the Light, Creating True Prosperity, *and* The Four Levels of Healing. *In the following dialogue, Shakti*

Gawain explores how to create physical, emotional, financial, and spiritual prosperity.

※ ※ ※

MICHAEL TOMS*: The word* prosperity *has many meanings. To one person it means one thing, to someone else, it means something different. How do we cut through to what it really means?*

SHAKTI GAWAIN: When I decided to write a book on prosperity, I interviewed many people and asked people in my workshops, "What is prosperity to you?" I was curious to find out what most people think. I got a wonderful variety of answers that helped me understand more of my own thoughts about it. But as you indicated earlier, *money* is what most people think of when you mention prosperity. We think that if we only had enough money, the right amount of money, it would make us feel secure or it would give us freedom. The word *freedom* also comes up a lot for people. They think, *If I could just have enough money to feel free, to not feel constrained by not having enough money so that I could do the things I want to do in life and have what I want.* They understand that money isn't necessarily the ultimate object of their desire, but most people do think that somehow having enough money will get us to what we really want. And, of course, in talking and thinking about this, I realized that we all know people who have lots of money—or certainly have a fairly good amount of money—who aren't really experiencing prosperity. In fact, most people, no matter what their income level, aren't experiencing a sense of prosperity.

We don't have the sense of freedom that allows us to do what we want to do—or the sense of security we long for. There's no amount of money, of course, that can really bring us that sense of security or that sense of freedom. In fact, it's ironic—the more money we make, the more complicated life tends to get. The more things we acquire, the more responsibilities we initiate. We have to manage the money, all the things we acquire, and somehow life gets stressful and complicated as we get more successful. And that feeling of freedom we thought we'd have isn't necessarily there.

I remember Joseph Campbell saying, "If you follow your bliss, you'll always have your bliss. If you follow money, you may lose it, and you won't have that." So when you get more money, you have to protect it and defend it. You have to worry that you may lose it.

There's a certain level of stress and difficulty that goes along with every level of income, and I've often observed people who have millions or even billions of dollars, and what are most of them doing? Most of them are working very hard to try to make more money. And the question becomes: How much is enough? Well, of course, at that point we're really talking about power, and we're really talking about a kind of competition that goes on among the richest people. Who's more powerful than whom? Who's the richest of all? But they are not feeling prosperous, and that gets back to the idea that at every level of income—from the poorest to the richest—very, very few people have a feeling or a sense of prosperity, at least not in the way we think we should have if we just had the right amount of money.

On the other hand, there are people at every level of income who *do* experience prosperity, who feel prosperous in their lives, or who feel a high degree of prosperity. There are people who lead very simple lives and feel a certain kind of contentment. I also know people who make quite a bit of money and who love what they're doing and live the way they want to live. So I came up with my working definition of true prosperity, which is: "Prosperity is the experience of having what we truly need and want in life." To me, that's the real factor that brings us prosperity—prosperity is an experience. It's not something that comes from anything really external.

The issue of having what you need and want means you need to be clear about what it is you need and want, or at least you need to focus on that and investigate that. Maybe we don't have to have absolute, perfect, crystal clarity, although it's nice when we do. It's certainly true that when we get very, very clear about what we really need and want in life, it tends to open a door. It tends to bring us what we want.

The more we're not really in touch with our deepest heart and soul needs, the more we think of all kinds of things that *might* make us happy or that *might* bring us satisfaction. These are what I call false cravings. You know, we have a craving for this, a craving for that. It's what our addictions are really all about. There are many things that we may not think of as addictions, but simply as things we long for and yearn for, thinking they'll make us happy, but they really don't have much to do with our truest, deepest needs and desires. So we need to start to pay attention. We need to say, "I'll look a little deeper to find out what it is that I'm truly longing for in my life."

True prosperity is related to all four of the levels of human experience: spiritual, mental, emotional, and physical. We have needs and deep desires on all of those levels. They all have to be fulfilled to some extent for us to experience a certain kind of fulfillment in life. As we develop and investigate those levels, we get really challenged in how we can create prosperity.

Let's go back to money. We relate to prosperity as money. Money is a mirror of what's going on in our life, but how is it a mirror?

First of all, I believe that everything in life is a mirror. Everything that has happened to us in our external life is, in fact, a reflection of what's going on in our consciousness. That's not a brand new idea, obviously. Many of us hold that idea. I believe that everything that happens can be a learning experience, and if we look at our external life as a reflection, we can use it to see better what's going on inside of us. It's hard to see what we're unconscious of, because we're unconscious, but we have this wonderful way of creating a reflection out in the external world that can then show us. Money is one of the very powerful mirrors and reflections that we have in our life.

When you think about it, what is money? It's pieces of paper; it's pieces of metal. It has no real intrinsic value. It's a symbol that we've agreed upon and created to represent energy. Creative energy. I use my creative energy in a certain way, I make money for it, and I take that money and pay somebody else for their creative energy. So money is really a symbol of how energy is moving and flowing. And that's what it can reflect to us in our own lives. If we listen to our intuitive inner sense of what we need to do, and we follow that and act on it, we experience a feeling of being in the flow. When we feel in the flow, chances are that the money in our life will be flowing fairly freely and smoothly. It doesn't make much difference how much money it is. We all have our own style and our own journey in that way. Some of us are here to learn to live a fairly simple life with not a lot of money. Some of us are here to learn what it is to manage large amounts of money. So how much money we have is not as important as knowing there will be enough for whatever we need when we're in the flow. That's usually how it works. If there is a problem about money, the mirror of our external life is usually trying to show us something that we need to become aware of in our own consciousness—some area of healing that's needed spiritually, mentally, or emotionally.

What does it mean to be in the flow?

To me, being in the flow means that we're connected to our intuitive sense of what's true and what's right for us. We're moving with the energy. It's always coming through us and trying to move us in the direction we need to go. When we're really moving with that energy, we have a sense of being right where we need to be, doing what we need to be doing—we're in the flow. And when for some reason we're not attuned to what's true or right for us—not trusting it, not acting on it, or not following it—we feel stuck, frustrated, and confused. That's all part of the cycle. I think we have to go through times like that. But from those times, we usually get taken to a deeper place and a deeper kind of healing.

Another term that is often associated with prosperity, is abundance. *There's this idea that somehow, if you're not living your life right, you* don't *have money. If you're living your life right, you* do *have money—and if you're thinking right, you should have abundance.*

I think there are three common viewpoints about money. One is the materialistic viewpoint. Another is the transcendent spiritual viewpoint. But the one you're talking about is what I call the "New Age" viewpoint. It has a lot of truth to it. It's basically saying that life is a reflection of consciousness, and as our consciousness grows, deepens, and expands, everything in our life grows—and that includes money and a sense of abundance. So there's a lot of truth in it, but it does tend to be taught in a way that is too general and simplistic. It tends to give us the idea that we'll have lots of money if we live right, and if we don't have lots of money, we have to wonder what's wrong with us.

I believe that each of us has a particular journey here in this life. We came here to learn certain things, to experience certain things. I don't believe that every one of us is meant to have vast amounts of money. As I said earlier, I think some of us are here to learn how to be happy with simple things and maybe with not a lot of money. So I don't like the notion that we must be doing something wrong if we're not experiencing incredible financial abundance. Our culture has gone so far in the direction of overusing, overspending, overconsuming, and in thinking that we need to have lots of money and lots of things, that I believe we're very much on a correctional course right now. A lot of us are realizing that all those things and all that money aren't as important as some of the simpler things or the deeper things in life.

It occurs to me that one of the things that often is problematical with questions such as What is prosperity? What is abundance? What is too little? What is too much? *is that our lives are so filled up that we don't even know how to start moving in the right direction. We're stressed because we don't have enough money. Or we're stressed because we can't meet an obligation. Or we're not in a position or a place in our life to really step back and look at it clearly. How do we change that?*

Our lives are so full and busy—so jam-packed—and we're always having to make choices between things. I think the number-one problem for most people in our culture, at this point, is that there is just too much. We're too stressed by it all. We feel we don't have time for contemplation; we don't have time to step back and look at the bigger picture. But life is always trying to get us to go in the direction we need to go for balance and wholeness, and sooner or later, if we don't take the time, it will be forced on us through an illness or something. So if we can manage to just take a bit of time here or there or go somewhere to get some help, to get some support, it can make such a difference. There are times when we really need the support of going to a group, a workshop, a church, or whatever. We all need to be reminded over and over again of those things that deep down inside we know, but we lose track of.

Sometimes we need the support of a group, but we have to be careful not to let that become another in a list of obligations that uses up our time. Sometimes we just need to sit by ourselves and reflect. One of the things I discuss in my book *Creating True Prosperity* is that it's the poverty of time that we experience. Many of us have more of a lack of prosperity in our time than we do in our money.

Life is filled with polarities and opposites. One pair of opposites involves energy—what I call *doing* energy and *being* energy. In our culture, most of us are better at doing. We've been taught that we should always be accomplishing something and producing something. We should be on target, heading toward a goal. A lot of us are really good at constantly driving ourselves in the direction of something productive, and we have lost sight of the fact that *being* is just as important. In fact, the more energy you expend in *doing*, the more drained you become if you do not allow yourself equal time for *being*. One of our big challenges is to see if we can own and develop and balance those polarities.

Jacob Needleman has written a book called Time and the Soul *in which he discusses the idea that we all want our time to become more meaningful because we have so little of it.* USA Today *did a survey showing that more and more people are looking for meaning and purpose in their work. It has to do with time. How are we spending our time, and what are we spending it on? Sometimes, it seems meaningless.*

When we lose touch with the deep *being* energy, everything we're doing starts losing meaning. I love my work; I love most of what I do in my life. It's very fulfilling to me. However, when I get too far out of the balance in the direction of doing, doing, doing, it doesn't matter how wonderful it is, I start to have this deep-down underlying feeling of pointlessness. I try to deny it at first, but when I start to feel that way, I've learned it's a message to me that I need some *being* time, or I need some more self-nurturing. I need to stop giving out and putting out and doing, and I need to start replenishing and taking in and nurturing myself.

Once we understand the difference, we can learn to shift from *doing* energy to *being* energy. We can play with it and learn how to bring in *being* energy. When we move into *being* energy, all of a sudden that long list of things that we thought were so essential to get done falls away. We can start to enjoy just being here in this moment. And suddenly we just get a whole different perspective, and interestingly, when we do that, very often those things get handled that we thought we had to rush out and do. Somehow it gets handled, or it waits until tomorrow.

The doorway to spirit and to soul is through *being*. If we can't take time to relax and get present with ourselves, we will not be able to access the deeper levels of our own experience. That's why all the religions and spiritual paths are always advocating being in the present moment. That's really what *being* energy does. It brings us into the present moment.

Do you think we ever get to the point where we can say, "Oh gee, there aren't any more problems now. I'm there; I've got it."

I don't experience it as being like that. To me, it's just a constantly deepening, expanding, ever more fascinating and maybe subtler process. But I don't think we ever get to a point where there are no more problems or no more issues at all. I have big problems and issues and challenges. Everybody I know does. Everybody who's on a personal growth path does, but that's the adventure of life. We didn't come here just to go from point A to point B, and suddenly everything becomes static. To me, it's an ongoing journey that keeps getting deeper, and every time we move to a deeper level, there's a whole new level of challenge ahead. We go through pain; we go through confusion. Sometimes, we think, *Oh my gosh, I thought I had it, and now I feel like I've lost it!* But that's always an indication that I'm just moving to a deeper level of my own unfolding.

I think we're just in an incredible place in consciousness in this world right now, where we're really working on integrating so many things, such as integrating the soul and the personality—integrating our spiritual, mental, emotional, and physical selves. We're learning to live in the physical world with a lot of awareness of all the levels. That's never been done before. We're pioneers here. I don't think there's anybody ahead of us on this path. We're really moving along, discovering a lot of incredible things. I expect that to go on throughout my lifetime and beyond.

Certainly, we've never faced the kinds of major problems in the world that we are facing now, and certainly we've never been aware of them as much as people are aware of them now because of the kind of communications technology we have.

People have always had serious problems, crises, and difficulties. It's just that now we're conscious on a global level, where before we were just focused on maybe our family or our tribe or our community or our nation. Now it really is fascinating how we are part of this global community and global consciousness, so our problems and challenges are on that level. Yes, they are very scary and intense, but I think that's what we need right now in order to wake up more, to become more conscious, and to bring ourselves into greater balance.

We're really in a time personally, individually, and collectively where we're facing our shadow. We're beginning to know all those things about ourselves, all those aspects of ourselves, that we've denied or been afraid of and swept under the rug or stuffed in the closet and hoped we wouldn't have to deal with. This is a time when we are being challenged individually to look at those shadow parts of ourselves and find out what we've denied and rejected, then we can begin to embrace and bring those shadow selves into our lives in an active way because they are parts that we need. Collectively, we're really being challenged with that, too.

The issues that are challenging us on the global level today or the national or community level are reflections of the same essential issues that each one of us must deal with individually. This world is made up of individuals, and the consciousness is really the same. We can look at the global issues or the issues that we're concerned about collectively, and begin to see how those come back to the exact challenges that each one of us is facing in our own consciousness journey. And the healing we can do on ourselves individually will affect the world.

How do you see what's happened in the last 20 years? Do you think we're making progress? Are we getting somewhere?

I only have my own life in a way as a reference. I just keep moving to deeper levels and integrating more and healing more. I see more and more people going through this process. People don't really enter the conscious personal growth process—where they know that's what they're doing and they are committed to that—until after they get really frustrated with living in a different way. They get frustrated with what they are doing and the way they are living, and eventually they—we—say, "There's got to be a more meaningful, purposeful way to live." At that point, we start exploring. I see more and more people doing that. It's becoming much more mainstream. It's a very rapidly evolving process.

As we work through these issues, these concerns, and deepen our own spiritual growth and look for true prosperity, there are a lot of competing voices that go on for all of us. We ask ourselves, "Do I really deserve that?" And maybe there's a voice that comes up and says, "Well, I don't know. Is that the way it is?" Maybe you can talk about that—how we can address those selves that come up.

Not only is that a very important part of life, but it is directly related to our experience of prosperity. We can only experience prosperity and fulfillment in life to the degree that we have gotten in touch with, owned and developed, and integrated all the different energies, the different archetypes, of life that we experience inside of ourselves. It's almost like having many different people living inside us. And each one of them has its own job and its own function. For example, my responsible self is there to make sure that I really take care of things that need to be done. My vulnerable self is there to make sure that I stay in touch with my emotions, my feelings, and my needs. There's also a child who wants to play. And then there's that critic inside who says, "Oh, I don't know about you." The critic may seem like a very negative part of us, but it's there to try to help us shape up and get our act together. It may have a negative way of going about it, but all of these selves within us have a purpose, and we need them all.

Becoming conscious of all of these selves is completely fascinating, and as I mentioned previously, one of the things that happens is that we become conscious of the ones that we identify strongly with, the ones that are running our lives. We also become conscious of the ones we've denied or disowned, and the ones we've shoved in the closet. Those are the ones that are very much a key to making our life work and bringing it into balance. When we begin to recognize what our denied or disowned shadow selves are, when we begin to make friends with them and bring them into our life, we find that they are like a magic key, unlocking doors of perception of which we were previously unaware. For example, if we identify strongly with being self-sufficient and together and powerful, we might be terrified of vulnerability because we don't want to open that up, but it will be the exact thing that will begin to bring our life meaning and heart and soul. Or if we're afraid of our power and have denied it, then we may find that in owning our power, we can really start to find purpose in life.

Most of us have been taught that it is more blessed to give than to receive, and deep down most of us feel that giving is better than receiving. We want to be good people, and we want to give a lot. To me, however, giving and receiving are part of the same cycle. If we can't receive as much as we can give, we stop the cycle. It's like breathing out and breathing in. If you can only breathe out, pretty soon you'll be dead. So I think giving and receiving equally is the most blessed state. We can allow ourselves to take in as much as we give out, but many of us identify strongly with being givers and doing good and helping others, and we don't necessarily allow ourselves to receive what life is trying to give us. That has a direct bearing on prosperity. If we can't receive, then we will again be running on empty; we won't be able to get the rewards of our experience. Finding that balance and developing it is very important. It's probably the most important building block of prosperity.

Going back to those individual parts of our self, it would seem that many people are not aware that we can actually have dialogues with these different selves. We can talk to them. We can interact with them, and really, they just want to be heard.

It's amazing to use the voice dialogue work that Hal and Sidra Stone created. You work with a facilitator, and the facilitator stimulates dialogues with some of the different parts of a person. It's truly amazing what happens when the voices come out. The different selves speak up. And they want to be heard. They want to be valued and appreciated for the hard work they are doing and the job that they do. When we begin to consciously recognize and acknowledge them and appreciate them, it's as if we can begin to have them all work together more. We can begin to contain the whole of who we are, which is quite expanded. It's one of the most powerful things in my life that I've ever done. I've brought it into my own work.

Why was it particularly powerful for you?

It's a process that gets so directly in touch with exactly what's going on inside of you—not somebody else's interpretation of it. You can hear the selves within you actually speak out and say, "What's going on?" It clears up an enormous amount, and it helps you begin to step in—in a conscious way—and take charge of the process. It has taught me great respect and appreciation for all aspects of human nature. Most of us think that there are certain parts that are good and certain parts that are bad; there are certain parts that are desirable and certain parts that aren't so desirable. And yes, maybe we have to tolerate and learn to love all parts of our self, but we really need all sides of ourselves. When we begin to actually learn to appreciate a part of our self that before we hated or feared and we begin to recognize it as a valuable part of our being, that's real self-love.

There is a contradiction that comes up sometimes—particularly when one is following very spiritual practices—that says, "Stay away from desires and wants. Watch out for them and be detached." But here we're suggesting that we can have what we want—we can have full prosperity, and so forth. How do we address this contradiction?

That's definitely one of the big conflicts that comes up for people when dealing with money, dealing with prosperity. There are all these conflicting messages. We've got the materialistic, advertising world saying to us, "You need all this stuff." Then, we've got traditional religions from the East and West, saying, "The material plane is in some ways a temptation away from true spiritual values." We have a lot of conflict about that. The problem with the traditional, transcendent focus is that there is a basic, underlying split. We are taught that the spiritual is what's true and what's worthy and what's best, but there's something about the human experience that's less than that. So, we need to get through this human experience as fast as we can, and rise above and transcend and get beyond it. That's the basic message in most of the Eastern and Western traditional spiritual paths. It's a subtle message that puts us in conflict with ourselves, and it doesn't really allow us to truly honor all aspects of who we are.

That giving is better than receiving, for example, is a subtle message most people have gotten. We think that the really virtuous people are those who only want to give and serve. What we do, then, is we deny the very important and necessary part of our human nature that has to do with taking care of ourselves and meeting our own needs—which is considered selfish. In reality, we need both of those. In order to be human beings on Earth, living in a fulfilling way, we need both parts of the cycle, and we need to honor them equally.

That conflict is often apparent where you see money associated with spiritual teachings. It has such a charge for so many people.

Again, because of that traditional viewpoint, money represents the materialistic focus. We need to realize that we don't have to go to an extreme here. We don't need to be totally materialistic. But trying to transcend and deny our human emotions and feelings and needs and our material, physical needs doesn't work either.

What about a spiritual practice? Do you have a spiritual practice yourself?

I have a number of spiritual practices. A spiritual practice to me is anything we do that helps us get into *being* energy in the present moment and thus able to access the deeper parts of ourselves. It allows us to have, at least momentarily, a feeling of being part of something larger and being in that flow. Probably the most important spiritual practice for me has to do with getting outside and being out in nature. Nature is filled with spirit, so it seems to help to be surrounded by a natural environment.

I try to take a walk or just sit outdoors whenever I can. I also have practiced Hatha yoga for about 25 years. I try to take a few minutes in the morning and do a little yoga, a little meditation. When I do so, it helps me center myself for the day. There are different things that come and go in my life. Probably the most important practice—I'm not sure if you'd call this a spiritual practice, probably a consciousness practice—is for me to first of all be aware of those different voices and energies inside of me as much as I can. Who's saying what and feeling what and doing what? I try to become aware of that intuitive feeling or sense of what's right for me at the moment.

What helps me, and what I advise others to do, is to sit down and relax and take a few deep breaths and think of dropping your consciousness out of your head and down into your heart or your solar plexus. Ask yourself, *What's your gut feeling at this moment?* We don't always understand it. Sometimes we have so many different emotions and thoughts and feelings going on that we can't sort it all out, but with practice we can usually begin to recognize the feeling. It's a different vibration from the other energies or voices.

It's not from the rational mind; it comes from the intuition. It usually helps to think of it coming from deeper in the body. Just try to listen for that or feel for that. And it doesn't usually give us specific information. We want it to say, "Well, you need to do this, then this will happen, and then it will all work out." But usually what you get is sort of an impulse to go forward or just wait or turn right or make this phone call or something like that.

It's important to have that quiet time to be able to listen. If we're racing around, it's difficult to hear that intuitive voice.

That's why I find getting outside and walking is so good. It establishes a kind of rhythm. We have trouble just sitting and meditating because we're so mentally active. It can take years, sometimes, to learn how to drop into a sitting meditation, whereas just taking a walk starts to put you into a reflective mode. There are many areas of our lives where we can tune in to that intuitive voice. Anything that helps us shift into *being* energy and gain access to the more spiritual part of ourselves, anything that allows us to focus on the present moment, becomes a spiritual practice.

Washing dishes can be a spiritual practice if you can focus your attention on what you are doing. That's the trick. A lot of people garden as a spiritual practice. They may not think of it that way, but it's the way they get connected to themselves. They go out and work with the earth and look at the plants, and they get into the present moment with it. It can be a wonderful spiritual practice. But if you go for a walk, or garden, or wash dishes, and you can only think of how little time you have and how much you have to do, you won't be having a spiritual practice. You'll just be having another stressful life experience. We just need a little time, a little focus, and that will balance out a lot of the stressful activities in our life, and it will give us the energy then to move forward with the things that we really want to do.

Do you find that more women gravitate to your ideas than men? And if so, why do you think that happens?

Although there are definitely men who are interested in these ideas, a greater percentage of women embrace them. Why is that? Well, that's a very good question. I think the kinds of things I deal with, looking inside ourselves, dealing with emotions and feelings, dealing with intuition and spirit, are traditionally easier for women. Historically and traditionally, women have been more supported in looking inside and being in touch with themselves in that way. Men have traditionally had to go out and deal with the world. Those traditions, while they're changing greatly, still have very deep roots in us. So I think it's easier for women. I think it takes a much more courageous man to enter into this kind of deep process. I also think that because I'm a woman, women tend to identify with me. Again it takes an interesting kind of man to be able to look to a woman as a leader or as an inspiration, although there are lots of men who can do so.

While it's true that men need to explore this aspect of themselves as much as women, it's important not to be judgmental about this. Often people get very upset. They want to know, "Where are the men, and why aren't they doing this?" I love it when there are men in my workshops. It definitely is very special and brings a certain kind of energy when there are more men and more male energy, and I really appreciate the men who do have the courage to do this. But I also really appreciate that we are coming out of a time where for many thousands of years—for the very survival of humanity—men have had to go out and do what had to be done in the external world to take care of themselves and their families. And that includes killing other people if they're threatening. And if you are going to be out there killing somebody and really protecting in that kind of way, you can't afford to be too in touch with your sensitive emotions and feelings. For men to do the job that they've had to do, it has been necessary to cut off a lot of their awareness and their feelings.

I know that women have been oppressed, but women have also been taken care of and have not had to go out there. Women have been free to explore the inner realms and the realms of relationship, and so we're better at it; it has become one of our strengths. But it's scary for men to do that. Just as it has been scary for women to step out into the world with power. We are now beginning to explore these opposite realms. Eventually, this will lead to each of us being able to attain true balance within ourselves—regardless of gender.

Are you optimistic about the future?

I have voices in me that are optimistic and voices in me that are pessimistic and afraid—just as all of us do. My strongest feeling about it is that I truly believe that what we are going through—

as frightening as it is and as many crises as we're facing—is what we need to do. It's all part of this shift in consciousness and this growth that we have to have. Ultimately, it will evolve and develop in the way that it needs to and is meant to.

⁂

EPILOGUE

Following the previous chapter about what is true wealth, personal growth pioneer Shakti Gawain also emphasizes the importance of fulfilling our hearts' and souls' longings as opposed to striving to make more money. She points out that we feel the lack of prosperity even when we have monetary wealth. Money is a mirror constantly reflecting us back to ourselves. It is a symbol of the ebb and flow of energy in our life. She suggests being in the flow through honoring our intuitive sense of what's appropriate and right for us.

Her approach is fresh and original. She dismantles the cause-and-effect relationship that most of us construct around money and happiness, and she challenges us to truly pay attention to our deepest desires, follow them to their source, and separate them from false wants and addictions.

Shakti explores and contrasts three traditional philosophies about wealth and prosperity: the materialistic approach, the transcendent spiritual view, and popular New Age philosophy. In the process, she reminds us how important it is to nurture ourselves. There needs to be a balance between doing and being. True prosperity embraces much more than how much money we have.

⁂ ⁂

CHAPTER SEVEN

Creating Financial Independence

Joe Dominguez and Vicki Robin, with Michael Toms

PROLOGUE

Recession, depression, the coming crash. The cashless society. Crushing credit card debt. A trillion-dollar federal deficit, living on borrowed time. The list of financial fears goes on and on in a society where money dominates so much of life. Consider that working to make a living may fill up half or more of one's daily life, and yet, even with all this emphasis on money and things financial, we seem to know very little about how money actually works, how it impacts our lives in many hidden ways.

The late Joe Dominguez (1938–1997) and Vicki Robin of the New Road Map Foundation represent two people whose lives exemplify their commitment to creating a new relationship with money. Joe Dominguez retired at the age of 30 in 1969—not through risky investments, but through working for ten years on Wall Street as a highly respected financial analyst and author of an internationally distributed weekly market letter. Since then, he and Vicki devoted all of their time and skills to humanitarian service. They took no money for anything they did. For many years, Joe Dominguez presented his seminar, "Transforming Your Relationship with Money and Achieving Financial Independence," internationally. In 1986, Joe donated to the New Road Map Foundation all rights to produce and distribute this increasingly popular seminar as an audiocassette workbook course so that more people could benefit from the program. Vicki Robin serves as president of the New Road Map Foundation. Joe and Vicki are also the authors of Your Money or Your Life.

In the following dialogue, Joe Dominguez and Vicki Robin take a look at money from a fresh perspective. They show us what it means, what it is, how it impacts our lives, and how we can develop and create a new relationship with it so that it no longer controls us.

❋ ❋ ❋

***MICHAEL TOMS**: How did the two of you come together? How did you meet?*

VICKI ROBIN: We met in 1969, and we had both actually left our jobs in New York City six months earlier, but for very different reasons. Joe had become financially independent. He had focused for ten years on the whole process of finding out what money is, designing a program for himself so that he could be financially independent. I had been a struggling actress, and my goal had been to be a producer and a theatrical director. I had stars in my eyes. I worked for two years in New York. The industry was very disillusioning. Before New York, I had worked with a theatrical company where I did everything—wrote, directed, and acted. It was thrilling to work with a group of people for a purpose that was larger than ourselves. But when I got to New York, it was everybody climbing all over each other to get to the top. I was very disillusioned with that. So I left New York, and I was looking for something else. During this time, I had accumulated quite a lot of savings, but I thought, *Well, I'll just spend it and see what's next.* I decided there must be something more to life than striving for the top. I had been voted most likely to succeed in my high school class, so I was very ambitious and success oriented. I was disappointed that the Big Apple wasn't what I thought it would be. Soon thereafter, I met Joe.

JOE DOMINGUEZ: The really bonding thing we both discovered was that although we had very different socioeconomic, philosophical, and spiritual backgrounds, we were at exactly the same point in our lives. We had played the game according to the rules, but there wasn't a payoff. We each had a sense of emptiness, a feeling that there had to be more to life than nine to five until you die. I had been questioning that for a bunch of years myself, and that's one of the main reasons that I left Wall Street. But then to meet somebody who was at exactly that point in her own life and who had also taken daring steps, leaving her career behind in order to find that something else, this had to be more than coincidence.

VICKI: At that time, Joe explained to me what he had done for himself. He had retired six months earlier and had no idea of teaching his method to anybody. But it makes a lot of sense to dispense with the money-making part of life as quickly as possible, because obviously that can't be the goal. There must be something more. When we talked about it, it made perfect sense to me. I had met many retired people in my travels. I'd visit national parks and hike and camp, looking for that something else in nature. And these retirees said to me, "Here I am. I can hardly see, I can't walk, I can't hike, I can't go down in the Grand Canyon. You're doing it right.

Retire at the beginning of your life. If I had known 20 years ago what I know now, I would have left the drugstore in Dubuque"—or whatever it was. So the idea had been planted in my mind that it would be possible to live free of that whole money-making, money-spending syndrome. And then I met Joe, invested my money, and was able to become financially independent.

Did you have goals other than becoming financially independent?

JOE: The intention was to have the freedom to search for purpose in our lives. And soon after we met, we began the dialogues that led us to the idea that maybe the name of the game is service. At that time it wasn't quite a cliché. I think it has become a kind of cliché. But reaching the top of the mountain isn't just about feeling good and having no problems. If you have no problems, take on some bigger ones—such as the planet's problems. That inspired us. And that's what we've been doing ever since. It's just fun. It's not out of a grandiose or megalomaniacal orientation. It just seems to be the way to go. It works.

In these times, we hear a lot about the pursuit of "right livelihood." You've been quoted as saying that what we need is less livelihood. What about the contrast of these two concepts? Here you are suggesting that we should give up a job and become financially independent, and yet there is this quest to find the right work, and frequently it is associated with money. The work involves money. What about that?

JOE: In talking to a lot of people over the last 20 years, I've found that it is fairly difficult to find meaningful work that pays—meaningful in the sense of truly serving the larger whole. I don't say that it's not theoretically possible to find it, but it's difficult. There are many occupations and endeavors that at first glance look as if they are service oriented. But when you scratch the surface, you find that they're as much a part of the problem as the solution. So that's half the story. And the other half is that we can rationalize anything we want. We can conclude that it's okay to take money for this and not notice we are selling out a little bit—and a little bit more. We want the security. Then, we reach the point where we say, "I better not rock the boat. I better not tell the boss." We end up back at square one. The supposedly serviceable job isn't one any longer. I've spoken to so many nurses who find this to be true. Doctors—who went into the profession because they truly wanted to help people—find that ten years into the profession helping people isn't their motivation anymore. That's the problem that I see. Money and power corrupt, and having to settle for a paycheck has the potential to corrupt.

VICKI: One of the things that is most powerful for me is this idea of disconnecting your work from your wages. Not that it's the right thing to do or the wrong thing to do, but just try it and see what appears when you start to separate those two things out. It's not necessarily true that if you are doing the universe's work, if you are doing your "right livelihood," you will get paid or rewarded in money. My sense is that when I'm doing my work, what I'm rewarded in is a sense of joy, of energization—not necessarily money. Energy that comes out of cooperating with life is not necessarily financial energy, and I think it is very useful to recognize that. Doing your right work may or may not produce income. If that's so, it may be necessary to produce income in another way.

There is another point I want to make here, too, amplifying what Joe suggests. There is a kind of denigration of the volunteer in our society. I worked as a volunteer on one project, and I interviewed many people. In the final interview, people were asked this question: What difference did it make to you that these interviews were being done by volunteers? Half the people said, "Well, we figured that if you could volunteer your time, we certainly could stay with the project. It was kind of honoring our time." The other half said, "Well, we knew they were probably working for somebody competent who had it together." In other words, a competent person was somebody who was making money or had a Ph.D. or the right qualifications.

We don't honor volunteering and voluntary work. Yet, my sense is that when you are doing something voluntarily, of your own free will, you can move wherever you are needed. You don't have to lock yourself in, and you don't have to form a for-profit corporation and get stuck for eight or ten years in seeing that through. You can work where you are needed and when you are needed, and if the work ever needs to stop, you can stop it in the middle and go on to the next thing. There is a kind of freedom and creativity and power that comes from volunteering that doesn't exist as much in paid employment.

JOE: Maybe the pay scale at the cutting edge isn't particularly good, but the leverage at the cutting edge *is* good. In other words, you are blessed by seeing that the world has a specific need at this point. However, you're not likely to receive a paycheck for pointing out and addressing that need. Yet, that's where the real payoff is—the payoff in terms of satisfaction and fulfillment, in terms of knowing that your life matters and that you are contributing. So, it's a trade-off. Is the nature of the contribution sufficient gratification? Is it fulfilling? Is the fact that I know I'm contributing fulfillment enough, or do I also need a paycheck? If the fulfillment is enough, then whether it's volunteering or not, money becomes a secondary issue. I think that's important.

A lot of people have the idea that achieving financial independence means having a lot of money—hundreds of thousands of dollars, even millions. What about that?

VICKI: For us, financial independence is having enough money to cover our real and perceived needs, wants, and desires. And it also means that the money is coming in on a regular basis so nothing that we do, we have to do for money. That's financial independence. Of course, then the question becomes: "How much is enough?" Few people have an idea of how much is enough money. It is *uncommon* sense these days, but it was *common* sense at one time, that there is a point of enough. Not deprivation. Not scrimping and saving, but there is a point where you have your needs met. You have a roof over your head, you are warm and you have comforts, you even have luxuries—and that something special you've always wanted. Whether it's a Mexican shawl or a Porsche, you are going to get value for the rest of your life for having had that luxury item. But you don't need ten of them. You don't have to keep doing that over and over again. So there is a point of enough.

Most people who follow the steps that Joe has outlined in his program have discovered that their level of enough is far below what they ordinarily think they need to survive. And that's just at the financial level, at the level of money, at having income. We've broadened out this whole idea of financial independence to take a look at something larger. For example, how financially independent is somebody who can't fix his car when it breaks down? How independent is somebody who doesn't know how to bake a cake without a cake mix? How independent is somebody who can't fix the plumbing, and so on. It is as if we are so disconnected from the material world that we don't even know where a toaster comes from. We become dependent upon money to handle our lives. We have to pay the butcher, the grocer, the chiropractor, our therapist. Every need that we have in this culture is mediated by money, because we've disconnected ourselves from our own independence.

JOE: We need to face life. We use money as a buffer between ourselves and life so that we don't have to experience life. We protect ourselves; we shield ourselves. How much damage is that doing? I'm not a psychologist, but I think it's doing damage. I have a strong suspicion that when a fellow looks at that broken toaster and knows he has no idea how to fix it, his self-esteem goes way down. Even though fix-it-ness is not in his milieu, he knows that his dad used to know how to fix it. All he can do is throw money at it, saying "Well, honey, we'll just throw it out and go buy a new one." But that doesn't assist the self-esteem. The current myth is that having more money means that we have greater worth. Might it not be working the other way? Are we actually taking away our sense of worth because we have money to throw at the problem?

VICKI: You lose your own sense of resourcefulness. If you can pay somebody else to do it, then you don't have to do it yourself. One thing has been very empowering for me. I grew up in a wealthy suburb of New York City, and I wanted for nothing. I was the type of person who always had money to handle problems, but I got out of college and did not know how to handle life. It was very disabling. I had my couple of years in New York. Then I met Joe, and I started to live at a very frugal level. For me it was thrilling and totally empowering. "Oh, you mean I'm allowed to pull that lever under the dashboard and the hood opens? And I'm allowed to look in there?" I learned auto mechanics. It was a transformative experience to be able to open the hood, analyze the problem, see that it was something very simple and fixable, and fix it myself. Ultimately, I rebuilt a motorcycle from a box of parts. It was a box of junk parts—a basket some kid had put in his basement after having taken the motorcycle apart and not being able to put it back together.

The point is, that was empowerment, that was financial independence—being able to kick over that motorcycle and know why it was running. That was a direct connection with the world. For me, that's worth a lot more than having $2,000 to buy myself a new motorcycle. That's what we mean when we talk about financial independence—self-reliance, resourcefulness, the sense that we can interact directly with the world and handle it.

Since we are talking about the world, what about people who want to travel? Money is usually necessary for that. How do you handle something like that?

JOE: You take some money and travel around the world. The problem here is that people think they need a lot more money than they actually need. We've talked to people who've traveled around the world with a backpack, meeting people at their own level. They come back and find that they've spent less for the entire trip than they would have spent living in the city. So it is perfectly possible. Whatever your desire is, it is perfectly possible.

A very close friend of ours thought that when she achieved financial independence, she had to give up her dream of world travel. She began to dedicate more and more of her life to service. Within a year or so, she got an offer to present a paper in Italy at an international conference. The promoter of the conference lived in Switzerland and invited her to come early and help because she had conference experience. Because she was a presenter at this conference, all her expenses were paid. She had a magnificent world trip and made money in the process. But she didn't do it for that purpose. That kind of thing happens all the time. So nothing gets canceled out. As a matter of fact, your scope of possibilities increases dramatically because you are not caught up in the very small box of the nine-to-five mentality.

VICKI: Most people have two weeks a year for vacation. They have no time to really research where to go, how to live cheaply, how to backpack. So they have to buy into a very expensive prepackaged tour in order to travel. This is another example of how when we are in that kind of work routine, money becomes essential to everything we do. When we can get out of that nine-to-five grind, all possibilities open up.

What are some of the tricks that enable you to live this kind of life?

JOE: I'd have to say that the first trick is to know what is enough. If you think that having more is what is going to produce happiness or contentment or any positive attribute, you will never get there. As soon as you get to what you now define as *more*, you find that it's not enough. There is no finite end point to *more*. In every seminar I've ever done, I've asked people in the audience how much money they would need to feel truly satisfied. No matter what the income level, the need was always 10 or 20 percent more than they had. So people who had $1,000 a month were saying $1,200 a month. Those who had $5,000 or $10,000 a month were saying $12,000 or $15,000. So, here's a game where you never get to the goal. It doesn't make sense. As Vicki indicated earlier, it's *uncommon sense*. So, the first trick is to find out what is enough. In the course—and in common sense—there are ways of doing that so you know what is enough in your life.

The second trick is to know what is flowing in your life in terms of money. It's appalling how many people have no idea how much money is coming in and going out of their lives. I often say in the seminar, considering how you treat a dollar bill—the indifference, the negative relationship, or sometimes almost a hatred—would you hang around you? Would a dollar bill hang around in your life? Of course not. It would flee. And that's most people's experience. Money just flies out of their lives. Maybe something needs to happen to change that so that we honor this thing that we are putting so much of our lives into getting. And yet we dishonor it. We call it filthy lucre. But is it? It is what we are trading our lives for. We need to change our attitude about money. Having enough is not in numerical tricks. It's not in what to invest or a specific way of accounting or a special type of little book to keep the accounting in. No, it's looking at how it is that we deal with this substance that we invest so much of our lives in.

There is also in our society the phenomenon of incredibly huge salaries in professional baseball, basketball, and football. We have these ballplayers who say, "Well, $3 million a year is not enough. And then they say, "Well, I signed a $4 million-per-year contract for five years—$20 million—and it's financial security." What is financial security? $20 million sounds like financial security to me. And still it is not enough. It is quite amazing.

VICKI: There was a study done of lottery winners by a professor in Florida. He did a survey of over 100 lottery winners. He found that over 90 percent of them were less happy six months after they won the lottery. It is because the money actually disturbed the whole ecology of their lives. Maybe the lottery winner used to be a clerk at K-Mart and was known by people who came every day. Or maybe the winner had been on a bowling league. But the winners gave up those things because now that they had money, they thought they should do things differently.

The two of you have done a lot of work with community service projects and projects related to the good of the planet. How does the way we spend money affect the world around us? Do you think that most of us are blind to the idea that what we do personally with our money has an effect on the world around us?

JOE: That's been one of my favorite topics in recent months. Maybe that's because for 20 years, I have lived at a very frugal level, and I have been conscious of the ripples that my finances have on the world. I hadn't thought about the fact that not everybody else realizes that anything they buy ultimately comes from the earth. As consumers, they are taking something out of the earth—nobody is causing clear-cutting except the people who use the products. There isn't a conspiracy on the part of loggers to wipe out forests. They are only responding to our demands. An article that I wrote recently I called "Pogonomics" because Pogo's famous words captured it all: "We have met the enemy. And he is us!"

Environmental problems, waste problems at the other end of the scale, global warming, oil crises, and wars—they all ultimately stem from our consumption. And since here in North America we are proportionately the largest consumers, it is our responsibility to be aware of how we are using those resources. We need to be as much aware of how we use that resource called a toaster as we are of that resource called a car. I haven't worked out the numbers, but maybe there are just as many BPUs of energy used in the process of manufacturing that toaster—mining the materials, creating the plastic for it, refining the nickel and chromium for the micron heating element, assembling it, packaging it in Styrofoam, and shipping it to Sears—as in a 500-mile car ride in a 1958 gas guzzler that averages eight miles per gallon. It could be. But we never think of that. Let's not drive; let's take the bus today. It all comes from the same place.

VICKI: For me, one of the most stunning experiences was attending a conference two years ago called The Globescope Pacific Assembly. It was the first public hearing in the United States that looked at the question of sustainable development, the findings of the World Commission on Environment and Development. There were commissioners from the U.N. Commission, heads of corporations, and the head of the Army Corps of Engineers. Important people from the First and Third World were there. What came out of that week-long conference was that the single most devastating effect on our planet is the way we consume in North America. If we do not cut our consumption in North America, no amount of population control in Third World countries, no amount of food relief, no amount of anything is going to make any difference.

I also realized that not only do we consume voraciously, but we set an example for other countries. We are creating expectations in people. People in China have been promised by the year 2000 that everybody will have a refrigerator. Computations about the CFCs in those refrigerators are phenomenal. But how can we say to people in China or in Africa, "Well, look, I know we have refrigerators, but you guys can't have them because it's bad for the planet." The only way that we are going to be able to make it through that narrow channel into the future is somehow by finding a way for North Americans to cut consumption. Exotic forms of service (such as going to an African village and helping them) are trivial compared with the service that we could provide here in North America. Somehow we need to make reducing consumption seem fun, doable, and a contribution to the planet. It's not just that we need to change our consumption habits, making them more environmentally safe. We need to stop being consumers—stop being a nation that uses, squanders, wastes, and destroys. We need to stop that destructive process called buying your way to happiness.

JOE: Dr. Robert Muller, the former Assistant Secretary General of the U.N.—to me, one of the great peacemakers of our time and a beautiful human being—wrote something that captures it all. After 40 years of working in the U.N. and being involved in every peacemaking operation, he said, "The single most important thing that any of us can do to help the earth is to return to frugality." We have to redeem the word *frugality*. That is almost considered a dirty word today. Somehow frugality has come to imply being cheap and depriving yourself. But what it really means is using our resources wisely and using common sense in how we spend our money.

When I used to advise people on an individual basis, so often the bottom line was that they hadn't really paid attention to what they were getting for an expenditure in terms of what it brought to them. Did it really bring fulfillment, or was it an act of conformity? "Well, everybody has to go out and buy a purple 'gazingus' pin—everybody on my block is doing it so that's what I'm going to do." But did it give satisfaction commensurate with the 11 hours of work that it required to make the purchase? Often, the answer was "I never thought of that." But that's what we have to think about. That automatically leads to frugality. We would be more conservative if we could see the link to our own energy.

Whatever we might think about the environment or the impact that our consumerism has on the earth (even if that's not meaningful to us), there is something that does have meaning—our own lives! It is our energy and our time that goes into making those purchases possible. Someone who is 40 years old has 260,000 hours of life left on an actuarial table. How will we use the 260,000 hours? How will we spend it? Well, if we spend 58 hours of it, including overtime, on a job, and then if we spend that 58 hours' worth of time on a *gazingus* pin, we'd better get that proportion of fulfillment from our purchase because we just gave up a pretty precious resource for it—our own life! But if we honor the resources of the earth and honor our own personal resources, this naturally will lead to a frugality.

VICKI: The other question that Joe asks people about their expenses—beyond "Did I get fulfillment commensurate with the amount of life energy I spent?"—is, "Was this expenditure in alignment with my values?" The question of value is important. Did I get good value? Did I get more bang for the buck? We need to ask ourselves, "Did buying this gazingus pin take me closer to what I say I value in life?"

I had people at a workshop do an exercise where they just took out their wallets and meditated on them. What's in there? What is this? I asked them what would be the most devastating thing to lose. For many people it was their credit card. Then I said, "If you had to take one thing out of your wallet and show it to the person sitting next to you that would best represent who you are, what would you take out?" And it was a picture of their family. It showed that how they spend their resources is not taking them any closer to a sense of fulfillment. As a matter of fact, very often it takes them farther away.

There is also the example of the absent father who works 80 hours a week and says he's doing it all for his family—but he does not experience being *with* his family. So, too, when we ask that question about our expenses, we start to align how we spend our money with what we really say is important. That is a good question for people who want to be environmentalists. A phenomenal percentage of the population now considers themselves environmentalists. So you start to ask, "Is the way I'm earning and spending my money in some way good for the environment?" That will naturally lead toward a reduction in consumption.

JOE: And an increase in fulfillment is important.

VICKI: I was talking recently with someone at Rocky Mountain Institute, and this person said after all the thinking and all the research, the conclusion was that what would be best for the environment would be if we could buy something durable and then never have to buy another one. It's the buying of the product repeatedly that is bad for the environment. We need to ask how we can align how we earn and spend our money with our values about the environment. One might, for example, select a good vacuum cleaner, keep it in good repair, and not ever have to buy one again. It is that kind of thinking. It is the implications of asking those questions that makes the changes. It's not a laundry list of ten items you are supposed to buy if you want to be a green consumer.

We live in a society that in many ways promotes consumerism, promotes buying more. Television is an example. We drive along the highway and see billboards. We turn on commercial radio and hear commercials. All these things say "Buy, buy, buy." So how does one disengage from a society where we are being constantly inundated with these messages to consume more?

JOE: Just say NO. If we want our kids, who are constantly being bombarded by peer-group pressure to do drugs and alcohol, to say NO, we have to be able to say it ourselves—we, too, need to withstand the pressures. That's the answer. We pride ourselves as a nation on being free thinkers and thinking for ourselves. Let's put it in action. And by the way, that is changing and it is very interesting. The *Wall Street Journal* dubbed the '90s the age of frugality in one of their headlines. Frugality is being redeemed. There are a lot of signs that we are returning. It is a cyclical thing. Let's face it—a good percentage of the population knows all of this. They are the folks who lived through the '30s. In our age of incredible wealth and overflow, we simply have forgotten these things. So we're not saying anything radically new.

VICKI: It was very empowering for me to learn the history of consumerism. We've been brought up to think of ourselves as consumers. I'm an American consumer. I exercise my rights as a citizen by consuming. That's actually the main benefit of the Bill of Rights. That's what we have over the planned economies. We can consume! It actually was something that came about in the 1920s. People noticed that the Industrial Revolution had been successful. We had set up all these mechanical slaves to provide for our needs, and by then our needs had been provided for. So people stopped buying things. And workers—instead of wanting to spend longer hours with these machines and make more money—wanted to spend more leisure time with their families. It appeared that the wheels of industry were going to stop. In an inspired move, the government and business got together in the 1920s and said, "Look, if we can educate people to want what they don't need, we can keep the machinery going." So when you start to find out that your urge to splurge is a by-product of being educated to want what you don't need so that the machines can keep running, you start to ask questions. It just takes a little education in marketing to know that what marketing is doing is trying to hook our fear, greed, desire to be special, need for approval, or if it is a non-profit organization, our anger. They play on our emotions so that we will exchange our money for their product. What they are really selling is the way that we are going to end the discomfort of feeling fearful, greedy, or not special. When we start to understand the basic rules of how this consumer culture operates, we can see it everywhere. And we can be inured to the pulls.

Are you subscribing to some giant conspiracy theory?

VICKI: It's not a negative thing. It was well meaning. It was a way to put people to work.

JOE: Almost any day you can find an article talking about how the American taxpayer, the American consumer, is tapped out. Consumer debt is outrageous. Across the page you'll find how the great white hope for an upturn in the economy is if the consumer goes out and consumes more. He can't consume more; he's tapped out. Obviously, the head of the business page, or the editorial board putting together the business page, didn't notice that gross disparity, that contradiction. No, it's not a conspiracy; it's a way of thinking—a very natural way of thinking. But it's gotten stuck. Like any paradigm, it may have worked, and it may have been a valid way to perceive things then, but times have changed. Gaia isn't saying, "No more of that." It's saying, "We don't have the landfill to keep on absorbing that. We don't have the atmosphere to keep on absorbing that. We don't have the ground water to keep on absorbing that." So we need a new message now, and we need new ways of dealing with a faltering economy. We cannot continue the rape of our resources.

Money is treated by many people as a taboo subject. Just about the most intimate question you can ask someone is, "Well, how much money do you make?" How do you feel about that question?

VICKI: I make about $600 a month—give or take $20.

JOE: I live on less than that. I average about $500 a month.

Why do you think it is such a taboo subject to talk about how much money you make?

JOE: It may well have to do with the link between self-esteem and our paychecks. We seem to live by the adage that "man is not searching for riches, but to be richer than the next man." I think Sweden or one of the Scandinavian countries published the salaries of all of their public employees, and people were outraged. This may, in part, be due to the association that we make between money and self-worth—money represents everything, including our masculinity. As a teenage boy, when you had $15 in your pocket and were going out for a date, you felt more virile than when you only had $1.50 and were only going for an ice cream cone. There's a lot of our identity that we, in this culture, wrap up with money.

In this day and age, how can people live on the small income that the two of you manage on?

JOE: The most logical answer is that I cannot conceive of living on more than that. Why is the burden of proof on me? How can anyone spend more than that? With all those thrift stores around?

What about housing? How is it that you can afford to own your home? Do you share it with others?

JOE: We do share it with others; it's a large house. That makes perfect sense environmentally. I think more important than answering that specifically, though, is knowing that we have a lot more dwellings in this country than we have family units to live in them. On top of that, as consumers, we're absolutely outrageous in terms of the square footage that we consider adequate for a single-family home. So once again it comes down to attitude. Some couples think they need to have a 3,000-square-foot home—I mean, that's bare minimum. Then, they have to fill it up with stuff. Of course, most people think they need at least $1,000 to make a rent or mortgage payment, and the $200 I pay out of my $500 sounds ridiculous in comparison.

We have to go back and ask ourselves why we set it up that way. That is the central issue. There are plenty of houses available for a lot less than what most people consider the norm. And I'm talking about good houses, not shacks. You can also pick your location. You don't have to live in one of the most expensive cities in the country. You are free to live in the most livable city in the country, as we are currently doing. At least they tell us Seattle's the most livable city, and we were able to find a house.

I live on $500 a month, but I sometimes have an income higher than $500 a month—like $600 a month. I put that money away because why would I want to spend it if what I'm spending is exactly the peak of my own fulfillment curve? It is exactly the amount that keeps me at that fine-tuned peak of personal contentment and fulfillment. Therefore, anything extra that I have coming in accumulates. I don't have to go out and spend it. Over the years, it keeps accumulating. When we decided to buy a house, the down payment was there. When I got together with several other financially independent people, we found that we could combine our accumulated savings into a gigantic down payment on a moderately priced house that was large enough for us. It was easy. But when somebody asks, "How can you live on $600 a month?" My answer is, "How can you live on any more than that?"

Doesn't somebody come around once in a while and say, "Gee, I'd like to have that"?

VICKI: Of course, if you are living under your income you always have money to have the thing that you think you want. I'll give you the example of clothes, because that's something that women traditionally like to buy. First of all, I shop in thrift stores, because in a thrift store you have infinite variety. If you go to your local Nordstrom's, you know that there are just a few styles you have to pick from. So I love it. I get great value from shopping in thrift stores. But also, I notice that the more clothes I have, the less I wear the ones that I do have. In other words, if I have three things, I wear each a third of the time; if I have ten things, I wear each a tenth of the time. So the clothes I really enjoyed, the more I got, the less I wore them. It just took a little bit of consciousness to come to that awareness. Then, I stopped buying clothes.

Do you have a car?

JOE: We bought a car ten years ago. We paid cash for it. We take good care of it, and it runs beautifully. We also have bicycles.

VICKI: We don't have to commute to work. We work out of our own home, so there's no commuting. I don't have to dress up in a different outfit every day of the month for the office. We eat simply. We enjoy each other's company so much that we don't have to go out and get entertained.

JOE: We have people over for dinner every night and enjoy human interaction. We've stopped using money as a buffer between ourselves and life. We don't ever spend money on entertainment. We've discovered that *we* are entertaining—humans are and life is.

⁂ ⁂ ⁂

EPILOGUE

The gift that comes from the work of the late Joe Dominguez and his partner, Vicki Robin, is the equation of money being equivalent to the life energy expended to generate it. According to them, we are still operating financially by the rules established during the Industrial Revolution, which were based on creating more material possessions. The facts are that our high standard of living has not led to a high quality of life, either for us or for the planet. Their financial road map suggests releasing the idea of "more is better," eliminating credit card bills and other debt, and, if we choose, to stop working for money.

Their admonition to figure out how much money we have earned in our lifetime to date, how much we're worth now, and how we spend our money, each and every dollar, will lead us to a heightened awareness of our actual relationship with money in place of our imagined one. Figuring out exactly how much time and money we spend to maintain our job enables us to determine our true hourly wage, so that when we spend money, we will know specifically how many hours of our life energy are being exchanged. The pot of gold at the end of the rainbow is financial independence and a sustainable living style, and each of us has the capacity to create this for ourselves.

❋ ❋ ❋   ❋ ❋ ❋

CHAPTER EIGHT

Money and Social Responsibility

Alan Reder and Michael Toms

PROLOGUE

Investors and investments have been with us since capitalism was born. The conventional wisdom is that profits, or the bottom line, are necessarily outside the realm of doing good or incompatible with the common good. However, during the past decade, a new and profitable form of investing has emerged that is beneficial to society and the planet. A direct result of the rising concern about peace, the environment, and human values, socially responsible investing, as it is called, includes a universe of investments that are not only beneficial to the planet but that can also earn returns as good or better than those earned by traditional investments. Alan Reder is a freelance writer and co-author with Jack Brill of a book entitled Investing from the Heart: A Guide to Socially Responsible Investments and Money Management, *as well as the author of two books on socially responsible business practices. In the following dialogue, he explores the world of socially responsible investing.*

❋ ❋ ❋

MICHAEL TOMS: *How do you define socially responsible investments versus other types of investments, such as traditional investments?*

ALAN REDER: In a general sense, socially responsible investing simply means investing according to both financial and ethical criteria. We don't ignore the financial criteria; we pay as much attention to them as anybody else involved in investing. However, for an investment to pass muster with us, it has to pass both financial and ethical tests.

To test financial investments in terms of ethics, you first need to determine what your ethical criteria are. You may be a single-issue person; that is, perhaps you are concerned about the environment or want to invest in a company that aggressively hires and promotes women or minorities. On the other hand, you may have a broad agenda that includes environmental issues, peace-related issues, labor issues, and so on. Any particular agenda that you bring to the table can be satisfied with this strategy.

There are many ways to approach this type of investing. You can certainly avoid putting money in places you don't want it to go, and there are particular strategies where you actually will do some very direct and specific social good by the investments you make. If you're concerned about weapons production, for example, you can screen from your portfolio companies that make weapons. There are very few people involved in socially responsible investing who will invest in a defense contract—or at least in a company that needs defense contracts to survive. There are about a dozen broadly screened mutual funds in socially responsible investing, and defense contracting is one of the criteria commonly screened out.

Treasury Bills seem to be the safest place to put your money. Where does the idea of social investment criteria come up around Treasury Bills? Is it part of that arena?

Treasury Bills are actually the antithesis of socially responsible investing because the money is not directed. In other words, treasury securities support the general activities of the United States government. Some government activities, related to education or the environment, might make ethically sound investments. But Treasury money also goes to tobacco subsidies, weapons production, and so on. The socially responsible investor who wants the same kind of financial security that a government bond can offer will step up to what are called agency bonds, which are tied to the activities of a specific agency. For example, the Student Loan Marketing Association issues bonds that support government-guaranteed student loans.

The Government National Mortgage Association (GNMA) offers securities that are involved with housing—single-family housing, affordable housing, and so on. These are called GNMAs, and they are a portion of the financial universe that offers some of the most popular investments because they give a good rate of return for a low level of risk. They are just slightly riskier than Treasury Securities, but they offer a better return than Treasury Securities, and many people feel that the difference in risk is more technical than real. GNMAs, then, offer another good ethical alternative to Treasury Bills.

How did you discover socially responsible investing?

I became aware of socially responsible investing long before I wrote the book *Investing from the Heart*, maybe as much as a decade or more before. I think I first read about it in a magazine that I now write for, *New Age Journal.* At that time, I had no money to invest or so I thought, but I was intrigued by it as a social activist strategy. I'm even more intrigued now that I know more about it.

The fact is, I could have started investing in a modest way, had I known more. Many people think that it takes a lot of money to begin investing, but that's not true. In our book, we show people how to start a socially responsible and financially astute investing program for as little as $25 a month. Socially responsible investing and money management begins with banking; therefore, if you have enough money to maintain a checking account, you can play this game. We show various kinds of banking institutions that will put your money to work for you in ways that give you more interest than you are going to earn in a conventional institution, as well as doing more direct social good and keeping your money from doing things that you don't want it to do.

For example, with $25 to open an account and an additional $25 a month, you could take out an account with the Franklin U.S. Government Securities Fund, which is a mutual fund invested in a GNMA. It's a safe, secure investment, not specifically socially responsible in that it hasn't been prepared as such by the socially responsible investment industry. But by definition, it is socially responsible in that it supports housing, which most people feel good about supporting.

What about companies that are on the stock exchange? Are any of them socially responsible companies?

Some of America's biggest corporations are fairly socially responsible. Stride-Rite is an excellent example. These people make the quality shoes that many of your listeners probably wore as kids. Stride-Rite has terrific employee benefits, such as a great family leave program. It has both elder care and child day care on-site. It has flexible time policies. It was one of the first companies to have a clean-air policy, which meant no smoking in any of the public and work areas. It is an outstanding company—socially responsible and profitable. Other companies of this caliber include Pitney Bowes, Rubbermaid, Quaker Oats, Dayton-Hudson, Church and Dwight, and many more. There are any number of companies that are basically good businesses with good people, and they want to do the right thing, ethically.

Beyond those are what I would call a tier of idealistic companies. One of the best known of these, of course, is Ben & Jerry's. Smith and Hawken would fit this bill, although they are not available right now as a stock because they are not publicly owned. Patagonia, Esprit, and Rhino Records are included in this group. There are about a dozen of these companies that really use their business as a way to do very direct social good in the world. It's a visionary concept.

The Council of Economic Priorities publishes a booklet about how to shop that gauges companies on their social responsibilities relative to shopping for their products. Are there other guides available for people who want to invest in socially responsible companies?

The booklet the council publishes, *Shopping for a Better World*, is also a good guide for investors. We actually used it as a resource for our book. The criteria the council uses are similar to those used by the socially responsible investing industry. If you use this booklet as an investing aid, one thing you have to keep in mind is that the company name you see on a product may not be the same as the parent company name. Since it's the parent company name that appears on the New York Stock Exchange, you'll need to find out what it is.

The Council of Economic Priorities also publishes an investing guide called *Investing for a Better World* that profiles companies. In our book, what we did as a guide to companies is create a resource that is fairly unprecedented in the field. We took all the socially responsible mutual funds and got the list of all the stocks they invest in. We alphabetized them, and next to each company's name we listed the various mutual funds that hold those stocks. Thus, you can get a sense of how they are regarded within the industry. It's a good starter list for picking socially responsible stocks.

How would you describe mutual funds from a socially responsible investment point of view?

There are about a dozen specifically socially responsible mutual funds with different kinds of financial strategies. Some of them are very cautious investments for people who are uneasy about putting their money at high risk or who are at a stage of life where it is not appropriate to be playing a high-rolling investing game. Then, there are more aggressive funds, such as the Calvert Ariel Appreciation Fund, an aggressive growth fund. There are also sector funds that invest in particular industries, such as the New Alternatives fund, which is a so-called environmental fund. It invests in alternative energy and conservation technology. Again, there are options for every conceivable investment strategy you might have. In every category of investment, there is a socially responsible option.

Do standard investment brokers handle socially responsible investments, or are there specialists who do this?

There are specialists who handle these investments, but conventional brokers do, also, because a lot of their clients come in asking for them. Sometimes what will happen is that a conventional investment broker will try to sell you a product, and if you investigate, you will find out that there is a socially responsible option that he or she didn't know about. This happened to me once on a cold call. An investment broker wanted to sell me an annuity from Metropolitan Life. I asked if they had a socially responsible option, and he said they didn't. But when he checked into it, he found that they did have one, and it was operated by Calvert, which is the largest operator of socially responsible mutual funds. Calvert put together a portfolio for Metropolitan Life, but it wasn't listed in the brochure; you had to ask for it. This is also something to consider if you work for a company that has a pension plan offering a number of options. You might ask if they have a socially responsible option because they might not identify it as such when they lay those options out in front of you.

What about planning for retirement? Are there some particular things to do from a socially responsible perspective that are better than other things?

When you are financially planning for retirement, what you are looking for generally is a conservative strategy to provide income for you to live on without putting your principal at risk—that is, the cash that you actually invest. This means that you are doing very little investing in the stock market. You are mostly investing in bonds or "debt" instruments such as GNMAs, which are a really popular retirement investment. That's a socially responsible option, but it's also a good idea to have a little bit in the stock market as a hedge against inflation. A good option there would be a mutual fund such as the Pax World Fund because it's half invested in conservative stocks—and by conservative, I mean from a risk standpoint, not from an activist standpoint—and half invested in bonds such as GNMAs. These are the types of things that people look for in retirement investing.

Another retirement strategy involves annuities. An annuity is an investment product offered only by insurance companies, and essentially it creates an income stream from the money that you deposit or the money that you invest. The insurance company takes that money and invests it, and it generates income that you receive after they take their cut. What some annuities do is actually just offer you investments in mutual funds through the annuity. The difference between investing in an annuity and investing in a mutual fund straight on is that if you invest in a normal mutual fund, you are going to have to pay taxes on any income you receive as you receive it. In an annuity, that income is part of a tax-deferred investment. So you won't pay taxes on it as the money is compounded. It is essentially a retirement vehicle; therefore, you pay taxes when you take the money out—at retirement age, ideally—much as you would with an IRA.

An annuity is a very complicated product. The age at which you can take money out and the amount you can withdraw are dependent upon the type of annuity plan you have. There are any number of different plans, and you need to make the arrangements you want with the insurance company.

What about certain credit cards? Are there credit cards that are more socially responsible than others?

There is some confusion about this issue. For example, the National Wildlife Federation, the Sierra Club, and similar organizations offer what they call affinity cards. The idea with an affinity card is that a certain percentage of the profits will go back to the Sierra Club or the National Wildlife Federation or whatever the affiliated organization may be. The problem with these credit cards, however, is that they are like any other credit card in that they are operated by big banks, and the money that the banks make generally does not go to socially responsible ends. There are only two so-called socially responsible credit cards. One is available through Working Assets, which is located in the San Francisco Bay area—although you can get that card anywhere in the country. The other socially responsible credit card is available through Co-Op America, which you can join for $20. But these organizations may also operate their cards in conjunction with banks you don't feel comfortable with, so investigate them before signing up. Are they better than the average credit card? In the ethical sense, at least modestly.

Many of the names, addresses, and organizations mentioned are in the book *Investing from the Heart*. We tried to make this the most comprehensive resource in the field without overwhelming people. We have not only included investment resources in the book, but if you want to investigate companies and organizations on the social side, we give you all the resources to do that as well.

There is a phrase that you use in the book called "social screening." How would you define that term?

Social screening is a phrase that basically applies to mutual funds. We previously established that socially responsible mutual funds are screened across a broad range of issues. Mutual funds concerned with environmental issues look for companies that either have a positive effect on the environment or, at least, are not heavy environmental polluters. More broadly screened funds also look for companies that are not involved in the military-industrial complex. They look for companies that treat their employees well, that hire and promote women and minorities, and that produce good-quality, safe products—safe for both the consumer and the environment.

When we talk about screening, we're talking about both positive and negative criteria. Negative criteria would be indicated, for example, by a company that does not terribly pollute the environment and does not treat its employees poorly. Conversely, positive criteria would be indicated by a company that does good things for the environment and that treats its employees very well.

There has been a dramatic increase in the socially responsible movement since 1985. How big would you say the movement is now, and why has the increase been so dramatic?

According to some current analyses, there is approximately $700 to $800 billion invested right now. The previous figure was $625 billion as of 1991. That was up from $500 billion in 1990, and up from only $40 billion in 1985. I think this increase has occurred because we're getting our point across. And our point, very simply, is that you can do as well by investing this way as you can with traditional investments—and often you can do better.

It has long been a prejudice in the field that if you invested according to ethical criteria, you had to give up profits; from a financial standpoint, that was not what you wanted to do. The feeling was that you'd be better off making as much money as you could investing in Phillip Morris, the tobacco company, or Lockheed, and giving what you wanted to charity. But we've shown that by ethically targeting your investments, you will do as well or better, and we can back this up statistically. In 1991, for example, the Standard and Poor's 500 Index was up 26.3 percent. The Standard and Poor's 500 is an index of 500 stocks, the performance of which is said to reflect the performance of the stock market as a whole. In the same year that it was up 26.3 percent, the Domini 400, which is an index of 400 socially screened stocks, was up 37.8 percent. It was dramatically better than the Standard and Poor's 500. That got a lot of people's attention and showed that what we said was true. Another thing that got a lot of people's attention was that in 1990 the Pax World Fund, which is one of the oldest and best of the socially responsible funds, was the leading mutual fund in its investment category—balanced funds—in the entire country.

What about the relationship between profits and performing ethically in the marketplace? There seems to be some kind of direct relationship that you discovered through the investment arena. Is there a direct connection?

This is a really fascinating aspect of socially responsible investing. It seems that the same process that allows you to identify an ethical company can also identify a company that's run better and is more profitable. We think that there's a direct relationship. Let me again use Stride-Rite as an example. Stride-Rite has strong family-leave programs, flexible time, and clean-air programs. Another thing Stride-Rite is well known for is maintaining its domestic labor force. In the early and mid-1980s, the shoe industry was very stressed by cheap foreign shoe wear that flooded the market. To meet that competition, many shoe companies went overseas looking for cheaper labor. Stride-Rite kept its labor force at home, where a large percentage of its work force is unionized. Did all these good deeds hurt Stride-Rite's bottom line? Apparently not. Stride-Rite's profits are about twice the industry average.

This really negates the claim of some corporations that when you do good things for your employees, you have to do it at a sacrifice to the bottom line. In fact, when you treat your employees well, they work harder for you, they do better quality work, and they stay on the job longer. Employee turnover is a major business expense, but when a company has flexible time programs, then there is not a lot of lost work time when an employee has to leave work early or arrive late because of a family emergency. The company operation already allows for that contingency, and it can save a large company hundreds of thousands of dollars or even millions of dollars a year, as studies have shown.

What is the relationship between the growth of the socially responsible investing movement and changing the world for the better?

I think that socially responsible investing is the most overlooked and perhaps the most potent social activist strategy available to us. Many of us are really dissatisfied with the political choices that are available to us, because we just don't see any politicians out there who can deliver the magnitude of change that we see is necessary. And the reason for that, of course, is because our politicians are more obligated to the corporations who pay their campaign bills than they are to us. With socially responsible investing, however, you can lean directly on the corporations and get them to change their behavior because money talks. Mutual funds sometimes hold hundreds of millions of dollars at a time in a single company, so when investors with that kind of power go to that company and say, "Look, we want you to become more environmentally positive before we invest in you," the company listens. The progress that we've seen in South Africa in the last couple of years is in a large part due to the socially responsible investors and investing institutions withdrawing their money from South Africa. They put pressure on the economy. Just imagine if all that financial power were focused on environmental issues or the issue of peaceful relations between nations or whatever. The potential is really quite phenomenal.

The Pax World Fund, which was actually the first such fund that focused on socially responsible investments, really came out of the Vietnam War, didn't it?

A group of Methodist churchgoers was looking for a way to invest funds without contributing to the Vietnam war effort. In response to that, a group of Methodist clergy put together the Pax World Fund. They have since added to its criteria so that it screens across the broad range of issues previously mentioned—labor, the environment, and so on. This fund performs very well financially. Over the last ten years, it has averaged about a 14 percent return per year.

There seems to be a lot of funds that talk about environmental purposes being at their core. Is it true that there are a lot of these funds?

You have to be really careful with the term *environmental*. Most of us have gotten cold calls or literature about environmental investments. The brokers making the calls make it sound as if you will make a lot of money by investing with them, and you'll also do good things for the environment. In such cases, it's important to remember that the technical definition of an environmental fund is simply a mutual fund that is invested in the environmental sector—in toxic waste cleanup, landfills, or pollution control equipment. Some of these "environmental" funds are actually invested in companies that have been cited for major environmental pollution and regulation violations. There are only two truly environmentally positive mutual funds. One of them is the New Alternatives Fund that I mentioned earlier, which is invested in alternative energy and conservation technology. The other one is the Shield Progressive Environmental Fund, which is invested in the environmental sector, but they screen out the really offensive polluters and otherwise look for companies that are good to their labor.

Investors really need to go beneath the surface in these areas and look for more depth of information. There is a stream of information coming from the socially responsible investing industry itself, and the concerned investor just needs to tap into it. Our book, *Investing from the Heart*, lists a number of publications available for the investor, including *Clean Yield*, which is a socially responsible investment advisor newsletter.

Ben & Jerry's is another company that's known as being innovative and socially responsible. How have they been innovative in what they have done with their company?

Ben & Jerry's, along with the Body Shop, which makes personal care products, is probably the preeminently socially responsible company in the world. The founders and owners are a couple of 41-year-old hippies from Vermont. I think they paid five dollars to take an extension course in how to make ice cream. They opened up a little store in an abandoned gas station, and now it's something like a $100 million company. They never lost the social values that they formed in the '60s, and they used their company in very ingenious ways to further their social goals. For example, rather than just buy the cheapest milk that's available to them from huge agribusinesses to make their ice cream, they support local farmers in Vermont. They actually buy milk at a premium from local dairies. Also, many of their ice cream flavors are tied to very specific social projects. For example, the brownies in their Fudge Brownie ice cream are made by a bakery that hires the homeless and other unskilled people. The blueberries in their Wild Maine Blueberry ice cream are purchased from an Iroquois reservation in Maine. The Rainbow Crunch ice cream contains nuts that were grown in Ecuador's rain forest; this provides Ecuador with an economically viable way to keep those trees standing as opposed to cutting them down. The company also gives away about 7.5 percent of its corporate profits to socially positive causes, and that is about four times the corporate average. And those are just a few of the things that make Ben & Jerry's an innovative, socially responsible company.

The Body Shop is the British equivalent of Ben & Jerry's in terms of their approach. They are also very active in their social ethics. They use the company as an engine to do social good in the world, and they make a lot of money. I believe their stock was first publicly offered in 1982, and ten years later, it's worth 100 times what it was from its first offering.

They, along with Ben & Jerry's and about 10 or 11 other companies, use space on their packaging to direct their consumers to specific socially positive actions. For instance, they may use the packaging to encourage customers to contact government representatives on an environmental bill or a bill related to promoting peace in the world. The Body Shop's personal care products are also cruelty free, which means they are not tested on animals.

In the 1970s, when Celestial Seasonings first appeared in the stores, it was such a novelty to see quotes on the package used to deliver messages. These were not necessarily activist messages, but they were quotes from famous people, literary figures, or poems. Then, it was innovative and new; now it's becoming almost standard.

The socially responsible companies, I think, are going to change the world of advertising. In 1991, a really fascinating ad was taken out in the *Utne Reader* by one of these idealistic companies. Esprit, the clothing manufacturer, took out an ad—I believe it was a full-page ad—that said, "Buy only what you need, but when you buy it, buy it from us." In the general business world, we would say these people are crazy. But when you really look into the future, this is where capitalism is headed. We operate on this infinite growth model, but the resources out there can't sustain it. We are using things up. If capitalism is going to survive as an economic system, it is going to have to adapt to sustainability. This is the message that Esprit pioneered.

I think that marketing and the marketplace will change radically because of social investment strategies. This is the real hidden financial promise of socially responsible investing. By supporting socially responsible companies with our investment dollars, we make it possible for them to become the dominant companies of the future, particularly when they are involved in sustainable industries. Companies involved in the alternative energy industry are examples of this; so are companies that build energy-efficient homes, make other energy-efficient products, or are involved in recycling. The companies that are going to shrink in the future are those involved with oil, nuclear power, and even conventional autos, because we can no longer afford the environmental cost of their products. The environmental degradation that we see all around us is going to be with us for a long, long time. Socially responsible investors are identifying companies that can address these environmental issues, and they're getting involved with such companies now. It is the socially responsible investors who will reap the profits when these industries skyrocket in the coming decades.

Are large companies such as General Electric, General Motors, Exxon, and Chevron going to be affected by socially responsible investing?

I definitely think that large companies are going to be affected by socially responsible investing. Most of these companies are so large that they are probably doing something that socially responsible investors don't approve of. Certainly the big auto manufacturers are all involved with heavy weapons manufacturing and other kinds of defense contracting. General Electric is a heavy nuclear weapons manufacturer and a lot of other things that none of us are too crazy about. Another reason these companies will be affected is because they tend to be big dinosaurs run by people who just cannot see the forest for the trees, so to speak. They just cannot see very far down the road. American business has been criticized for its lack of vision, for its inability to adapt to changing conditions, and the biggest companies are the main offenders. We look, of course, at the auto industry and see that they've been foisting lousy products on the American marketplace for years. They did it knowingly. Then, Toyota showed up. Honda showed up. Both companies offered cars vastly superior to the American counterparts, and American consumers switched over en masse because they were fed up. But American auto companies still don't seem to get the connection. Even now, when they are trying to compete with the Japanese more directly and offer better quality, they still don't come close in satisfying consumers or repair frequency. The real vision out there and the social responsibility, too, tends to be with the smaller companies that are more focused on a particular product.

Do you see investors moving away from companies like this and moving more to socially responsible companies? Is that going to be a trend?

Investors looking for long-term investments will be looking at socially responsible companies. On the other hand, people who look at the stock market as a casino have a whole different set of criteria by which they invest funds. In *Investing from the Heart,* we advise against taking the short-term view, because the chances of losing are at least as good as the chances of winning. If you take the long-term perspective on your investments, which is the wisest way to go and is almost sure to pay off if you do as we advise, then looking to ethical companies that have some kind of a vision and that are more in touch with their marketplace is the best strategy, we think.

What is the connection between social and political activism and socially responsible investing?

There is a way to directly use investing as a tool to make very focused political change. This is the technique of shareholder activism, which was pioneered by Ralph Nader in the early 1970s with his auto campaigns. When you own a share of stock, you have a vote. Every share of stock you own is a vote that you can register with the corporation at its annual meeting. In the '70s, you could also propose resolutions that the entire shareholder body voted on, so Ralph Nader and his people just bought shares in General Motors and used them as leverage to stop unethical activities. The rules have tightened up since then because so many of these shareholder resolutions were proposed that the big corporations went running to the Securities Exchange Commission and said, "Please tighten up the rules so we don't have to deal with this stuff." As a result, you now have to own $1,000 worth of stock for a year and a half before an annual meeting in order to write a shareholder resolution. But there still are a lot of people out there who meet those criteria and who want to effect change on the corporate level. So, for example, somebody who owns stock in a cosmetics manufacturing company may go to People for the Ethical Treatment of Animals and say, "Will you please write a shareholder resolution using my stock as your financial base, and let's get some good done here." Large companies such as Revlon and Avon have stopped animal testing because of the pressure brought through shareholder resolutions. That is one very direct way to make an impact with an investment.

Probably the most obvious example of shareholder dissatisfaction is South Africa, where people pressured companies to withdraw. We in the socially responsible movement encouraged investors to keep their money away from South Africa until black South Africans got the vote and other reforms were made.

Where you put your money is an effective way to express your view in the world. It is a very powerful activist strategy. Socially responsible mutual funds, for example, can hold tens of millions of dollars—in some cases, hundreds of millions of dollars—in stocks. If people realized what a powerful social tool this was, and also realized why, for financial reasons, they should start investing, then a lot more money would flow into these funds. And maybe instead of mutual funds totaling in the millions, they might total in the billions. So, when you, as a representative of a socially responsible mutual fund, show up at Dow Corning, for example, and say, "Now, before I invest in you, I want you to change such and such a thing," they are going to listen pretty directly because they want that money invested in their company.

One of the things suggested in the book is not keeping your money in a savings account in a bank, but in a credit union. Why is that?

What banks do with your deposits is invest them and make money off those investments. That is one of their main sources of revenue, and they invest that money without regard to ethical criteria. The largest banks will also loan money to foreign governments regardless of the human rights records or the form of government involved. So, by taking your money out of a bank, first of all, you are withdrawing your money from that unethical system. By putting your money in a credit union, you do a number of things. First, in a credit union, most of the money just circulates among the depositors. It is simply loaned out to other members of the credit union and is not generally put into outside investments. A credit union is kind of like neighbor helping neighbor. The interesting financial side is that if you have the same $100,000 of deposit insurance that you would in a conventional bank or savings and loan, you are going to get higher interest on your deposits, and when you need to borrow money yourself, you are going to pay lower interest on your loans because the credit union is a nonprofit financial institution.

There is a way of investing in a credit union, getting all the benefits previously mentioned, and doing even more directed social good. For example, in some communities, there are community development credit unions (CDCUs) that help the disadvantaged. What happens in these credit unions—again, because it's neighbor helping neighbor—is that the money you deposit there gets loaned out to people in disadvantaged communities for home loans or for small business loans, which then creates jobs in these communities. It's a way of helping these communities become more economically viable, and a way of using your money for social good. This type of credit union does the kind of work in disadvantaged communities that the government ought to do.

If you don't have a CDCU close to you, you may not find it convenient to use for your everyday banking. In that case, you could do your everyday banking in a credit union in your neighborhood, but when you need to take out a certificate of deposit, for example, you could use a CDCU. That way, you can ensure that your money is working for you and for the community.

Is life insurance a good investment?

Life insurance is a better investment than it used to be. Essentially, life insurance is for people who do not have a substantial estate, that is, a portfolio of investments, in place. Ideally, your investment portfolio is broad enough and extensive enough to insure you against the loss of a wage earner in your family, and you won't need a life insurance product at all. If you do need a life insurance product, we generally recommend that you get term insurance, which is the cheapest form of insurance, and then *invest* the rest of your money elsewhere.

If you don't have the discipline to invest regularly, a good option is universal life insurance. This is a combination of term insurance and investment. We do list some socially responsible universal life options in the book. What you get there is a modest but still market-level investment along with your insurance product. What you want to avoid is what is called *whole life insurance*, which is really kind of a ruse by the insurance company. The insurance company sells it to you as an investment product, but it's a very poor quality investment. You can do much better. If you are going to make an insurance investment, you should make it in the form of a universal life insurance policy and use one of the options listed in our book.

How has your own life changed since you started using socially responsible investments? Has it worked for you? Has it been successful?

I'm very satisfied with my investments. Of course, as I mentioned previously, when I first knew about this field, I didn't believe I had money to invest. I didn't realize how cheaply investing could be done. But in 1988, when my mother and last surviving parent died, I inherited a portfolio of investments that I converted to socially responsible investments. I am very satisfied with how they are performing.

I think this is generally the case among investors in this area. There are, of course, good products and bad products within the socially responsible investment universe, as in any group of investments. Some investments are better than others. I won't say that you can't go wrong if you follow the general advice in the field, but the percentages are certainly on your side. In investing, we are required by the SEC to say that past performance is neither a guarantee of future profits nor a predictor of future profits. Nevertheless, you can look at the long-term performance in the history of some of these funds and feel pretty good about what your money might to do for you financially. Do be aware, though, that even supposedly sure things can go in the tank. That's why investments offer more than banks. You accept risk for the possibility of higher returns.

With the aid of the book Investing from the Heart, *are you capable of going out on your own, or should you have a financial advisor? When should a financial advisor come into play?*

Using a financial advisor is really the easiest way to go. The bottom line is finding somebody you can trust. In *Investing from the Heart*, we show how to find both a socially responsible investment advisor and a trustworthy investment advisor. We are also quite aware that many people, particularly people who are attracted to ethical investments, are distrustful of high finance in general. They often feel better making these decisions themselves. If that's the way you want to go, we show you how to put together your own financial plan and do your own investing, even if you know nothing about it in the beginning.

What about tax considerations? How does that come into play with socially responsible investing? Is there a way to reduce your taxes through this mechanism?

If you are in a high tax bracket and are looking for tax-advantaged investments, one of the first places that all investors go are municipal bonds, which turn out to be, for the most part, socially responsible investments almost by definition because they do things such as build schools, parks, and libraries. Some municipal bonds also do things such as build prisons and dams, which not all of us feel good about. Therefore, if you are going to invest in municipal bonds individually, you are going to want to select the types of projects you can support. Municipal bonds, by the way, are the kinds of things that you see on the ballot: school bond issues, park issues, water projects, and so forth. Again, if you are going to get involved in a municipal bond mutual fund, you might want to take a look at what it's holding, although those holdings are going to shift from time to time. You may not be able to get a 100 percent ethical portfolio. At about the time we turned in the manuscript for *Investing from the Heart*, a new municipal bond mutual fund came on the market for California investors called the Muir Investment Trust, which does screen municipal bonds for social criteria. The Muir Trust invests mainly in education bonds, rapid transit, and that kind of thing.

The advantage here is that these are generally state and federal tax free, and even local tax free in some cases. In California, they would be double tax free, which means state and federal taxes. And this brings up another interesting point because there are a lot of people who don't necessarily meet the normal investment criteria for investing in municipal bonds in that they are not necessarily in a high tax bracket, but they don't feel very good about what the government does with their money. They don't like the fact that 40 percent of their taxes go to the military budget, and so on. And they would like to reduce their taxes for ethical reasons. One of the ways to do that is to invest in municipal bonds because you are not going to be taxed on your gains. You are going to give up a little bit in terms of return, because there is always a trade-off in investing. If you are going to get a tax advantage, you are going to get a little bit less return, but it is still a solid return compared with what you might get in a savings account in a bank or even these days in a money market fund.

The time for socially responsible investing is now; it's good for the investor, and it's good for the community. To put the concept as succinctly as possible, I would say that to create a better world, invest in it.

⁂

EPILOGUE

When we have financial resources and money, Reder tells us that it is important where we put our money. Dominguez and Robin suggested U.S. Treasury Bonds. Reder talks about socially responsible investments in companies and/or funds that are working actively to be responsible corporate citizens. If we want to create a better world, we must direct our money toward companies and institutions whose actions we support. Incorporating our ethics and moral values into any decisions about where to invest our money is crucial to the future of our society and the planet, according to Reder. He points out that the performance of socially responsible investments is equal to or better than other types of investments and can serve whatever goal we may have for allocating our money.

⁂ ⁂

CHAPTER NINE

The Future of Money

Bernard Lietaer and Michael Toms

PROLOGUE

Once in a century or two, something occurs to dramatically change the current of the cultural river. Everything shifts. Our worldview is radically altered. Our basic values, social standards, politics, and institutions are transformed beyond recognition. This is such a time. Call it the new Renaissance, the green revolution, the emerging culture—whatever its name, there is no doubt that it will change the way the world works. Not the least of this radical shift will involve the economic system and how we relate to money. In this dialogue, Bernard Lietaer will help us explore these monetary mysteries, and perhaps help us catch a glimpse of the birth of a new money standard far beyond anything we might have previously imagined.

Bernard Lietaer has been an engineer, a university professor, a currency trader, and a fund manager. He has also served as head of the Organization and Electronic Data Processing Department at the National Bank of Belgium, known as the Central Bank, roughly equivalent to our Federal Reserve System. Currently, he is a research fellow at the Center for Sustainable Resources at the University of California-Berkeley, and a visiting professor in the psychology department at Sonoma State University.

⁂

MICHAEL TOMS: *I think a good place to begin would be with an overview of the history of money. When did the use of money really begin?*

BERNARD LIETAER: No one really knows when the use of money began. It is lost in the mists of time. One of the most intriguing statements on that topic was by John Maynard Keyes, one of the best-known economists of our century. He said that money went back much farther than we've been led to believe by historians. He believes it went back to between the ice ages. He talks about the Hesperides and Atlantis—the mythical past.

From a historical viewpoint, however, we know that money systems were already developed in the Sumerian culture around 3,200 B.C., and quite sophisticated banks had developed as well. In fact, people learned to write not for the purpose of writing love letters, but to do accounting. The oldest texts we have are bank accounts, and they date back to 3,100 B.C. It's very interesting that several cultures around the world actually began using money before beginning to write—and actually began writing because of the money, not the reverse.

Money has been around a long time. We might think that banking started with the Rothschilds, but banks actually predated medieval Europe.

The oldest bank that we know of was Babylonian and was incorporated in 700 B.C. The scholar who worked on that particular decoding concluded that we haven't done anything in 19th or 20th century banking that they weren't already doing. So banking is a very, very old concept. We lost a good deal of it, by the way. It had no continuity between Babylonia and today. With the collapse of Rome, around the 5th century A.D., the currency system fell apart, and by approximately the 7th or 8th century, there was no system left. Everybody had his own way of doing things, which had nothing to do with banking. There were many little fiefdoms, and each lord had his own currency.

Is it true that the dark ages were partially caused because there was no money?

That's not actually correct. Interestingly, the money system that was used during the Middle Ages had something in common with the Egyptian system, and that is, there were actually negative interest rates on the currency. Normally, when you have a bank account, you receive payment for keeping your money in that bank. It's called interest. Now, imagine a system in which you are penalized for keeping your values in money. This isn't inflation or depreciation of the currency. It's a system where you are charged something every month for keeping your money in a particular bank. By doing that, you reverse the entire attitude toward money. Money becomes a pure medium of exchange, as opposed to a store of value. That has very positive implications, by the way, and could give us solutions to some of the problems we are facing today.

The lords that issued the currency had a system. In Latin they call it *Renovatio Monetae,* the renewal of the currency. Periodically, they would withdraw the money and issue new money, and there would be a tax in between. So you had people trading in currency, but you didn't have people storing value in currencies. If you were given $1,000, the first thing you would say is, "All right, what can I invest it in that's real and grows?" And you might decide to irrigate part of your land or plant trees somewhere. Currency was used only for trading. Today we do both things. We store value in currency, and we trade in currency. So there is an incentive today to accumulate wealth in the form of money.

There wasn't so much a flow of money as there was a flow of goods and barter. How did it work?

That's not entirely accurate. A barter system means living without money, making an exchange of goods for goods. What I'm referring to is people using money purely as a means of exchange. Money has different functions. One function, for example, would be storing value for your children's education. You create a trust account, and you accumulate money there. But in the money system I'm referring to, what you would do is plant a forest, because the money system at that time had a charge instead of positive interest.

So what we're dealing with is the nature of whether money is being accumulated or whether it is flowing.

If money is flowing, it's healthy money, a healthy system. The Chinese ideogram for money is a spring, the same as a water spring. Actually, currency comes from the word *current*, which is a flow. Money is, in that sense, a little like blood. If you have blood accumulating in one place, guess what? It's not a good sign. Something is going to go wrong. The blood should circulate, and money should circulate.

These days we do, in some sense, accumulate money. There are people who make money on money. There's this whole new field or profession of making money on money because we've become more of a global society where currencies are traded every day.

Currencies have always been traded. It's the scale that's new. The current volume of foreign exchange trading is about $2 trillion per day for a normal day. That's about 100 times bigger volume than all the stock markets being traded every day—a totally different scale. In the 1970s, trading currency might have been $10 to $20 billion on a normal day. We've gone up by a factor of 100 in less than two decades. So currency trading has become a major factor, and it has dwarfed the rest of the economy.

In some sense, money has become nonproductive.

Thomas Aquinas would agree. He didn't think money should have interest, because that's not productive. But I don't think productivity is really the issue here. The main function of money, in my opinion, is as a medium of exchange. Things go wrong when it stops being effective as a medium of exchange. That's when a money system breaks down. The difficulty is that when speculation gets beyond a certain level, which I think it has at this point, you don't have a measuring stick anymore. Everything becomes so volatile, so unpredictable, that you basically don't have a medium of exchange that you can rely on anymore. That's the real problem. I'm not saying that speculation is bad. I'm not making a moral judgment on speculative activity; some speculation is useful. Some speculation is necessary to have a fluid market, and it improves the depth of the market. But currently, the tail is wagging the dog.

In other words, only 2 percent of the $2 trillion of foreign exchange represents the trade of all the goods and services in the world. When an economy imports or exports cars from Japan or when a tourist takes a trip to Mexico, that actually involves dealing in foreign exchange. These are transactions that need to occur. This is what I call the real economy; real goods and real services are being exchanged. But only 2 percent of the total volume is now of that nature, while 98 percent is speculative. When the tail becomes 98 percent and the dog 2 percent, I think there's a problem. A tail is useful for a dog, but it shouldn't take that proportion. It is a question of scale.

When we talk about making money, most of us think of doing something to make money. But in fact, there's really a deeper mystery about how money gets created in this society, and it has to do with the Federal Reserve System, which seems to be made up of bankers who decide how much the money costs, how the money gets doled out, and how much is in circulation. To most of us, the Federal Reserve System is a mystery. What is the secret of modern money, and how does it come into being?

The current representative of the United States at the International Monetary Fund gave the following answer: "Money is magic. Central banks are magicians. Like magicians of old, they don't like to explain their secrets." So we are dealing with the mystery of magic, which has been part of the money system forever. These days, it is effectively hidden behind equations and arcane conversations that only initiates understand. The use of money involves trust, and trust is engendered by the use of symbols and reassurances. It's not entirely accidental that the money system is shrouded in mystery.

To help unravel the mystery, we need to understand that money is not a thing. It appears to be a thing. It has appeared for many,

many centuries to be a thing, but it's not a thing. Money lives in the same space as political parties, as marriages. It lives in the space of agreements. Money is an agreement within a community to use something (just about anything will do) as a medium of exchange. The key words are agreement, community, and medium of exchange. An agreement is a way by which, consciously or unconsciously, freely or coercively, we choose a particular symbol as a medium of exchange. Fundamentally, that's what money is—an agreement. When I give you a pen and you go off to a desert island, you still have a pen. It still functions as a pen. A cup of water is still a cup of water. But when I give you money and you arrive on a desert island, it stops being money. It becomes a piece of paper or a piece of metal or a piece of bronze or a piece of gold. But it's not money, because on a desert island, the agreement becomes meaningless. That's the first secret to unraveling the mystery.

Money implies relationships, not just a one-to-one relationship, but a community relationship in which the medium of exchange is acceptable to all. The community could be a group of friends who meet to play cards and use tokens as money. The community could be a temporary one, such as soldiers on the war front. They might use cigarettes as a medium of exchange. Or it could be the world community in which an exchange agreement is reached by treaty. The Bretton Woods agreement in 1945 made the dollar acceptable reserve currency worldwide.

Another aspect of money that we need to understand is the concept of ownership. You cannot talk about money as being *your* money. That's a little like talking about your marriage as being *your* marriage. Guess what? Your spouse is involved. You can't really talk about it without having the two parties involved. The same thing is true with money. Money is an asset to you as a medium of exchange only because it's a liability to the banking system. In other words, the secret is having a bank IOU that's acceptable as a medium of exchange to others. Money, then, is created from a two-party bipartisan agreement—mostly unconscious, by the way—between the banking system and you.

People usually believe that money is created when it rolls off the presses because that's what they see on TV programs—a machine printing all those dollar bills. You can have as many paper dollars as you want, as long as there is money in your bank account. You go to your bank branch and say, "Give me $100." The bank teller looks up your account (or the ATM looks up your account) and says, "Well, you have a balance that is higher than that. Here is the $100." You can do that as many times as you want, as long as there is "money in your account."

The day that there is no money in your account, you won't get the paper stuff. You can only get the paper as long as the computer says that you have enough in your account. But where does the money in your account come from? In most cases, you receive money from your employer. You provide a service, and you get paid for it. But where did your employer get the money?

The actual origin of money is in a loan. If you want a mortgage loan, you go to a bank. The banker might look at you and say, "Well, you want $100,000 dollars. You look like a serious, productive person. You look like you're going to be successful and therefore able to bring back the money when you need to. So we'll give you the loan." The value of the loan will be based to some extent on the building, but to a greater extent it will be based on you. In the case of corporations, it's not the buildings they are mortgaging. The building is not worth a lot. Microsoft, for example, is not mortgaging its buildings, and it has no problem raising billions of dollars in loans if it needs to.

The money that is created when you get a mortgage loan is actually created out of nothing at that point. The bank will credit your account for $100,000, but that money did not exist the minute before you were credited. That is when the money is created. Every dollar that you've ever seen, whether it is physical bills or in a bank account, has its origin as a loan to someone through the banking system. That's the origin of money.

It's important to know where money comes from because it highlights the fact that the banking system is a necessary part of the agreement—just as your spouse is a relevant part of your marriage. National currencies are always expressed by banks, so without the banks, the marriage wouldn't be able to exist. This form of money would not exist.

So when we have a monetary crisis such as we had in Mexico in 1994–1995 and in Asia in 1997, it's because the banks are in trouble. If the banks are in trouble, the whole society faces a potential crash.

When people lose trust in their money, they lose trust in their own society. That's on a philosophical level. On a very pragmatic level, when banks get in trouble, the first thing they need to do is call back the loans, and that affects businesses. So it starts with a banking crisis, but it ends up spreading through every single business in the country. Suddenly, everybody has money pulled out from under them, and a whole chain of events occurs. Companies have to fire people, or they go bankrupt and jobs are lost. That's why banking is really a very different business from any other service business, because it affects everything else. It is the means by which the entire economic system operates. So it is critical.

In your research on money and the history of money, you've come up with your own approach as to how money has worked over the centuries. Can you describe it for us and tell us what it means to you?

The money system was initially a reflection of the Great Mother archetype. Money was invented based on that concept. The very first coins, for example, the Sumerian coins, were tokens, depicting a bushel of wheat on one side, and a figure of Ishtar, the Goddess of Life and Death, on the other. The tokens proved that you had paid your dues in wheat, and they gave you access to the sacred prostitutes in the temple, for the ritual of fertility at the festival. Prostitution had a different meaning then. At that time, it was intercourse with the Goddess herself, and that was nothing to be taken lightly. Fertility was a question of life or death.

The origins of money had to do with the feminine energy, but over the years, that aspect of it was repressed. We know that whenever a particular archetype is repressed, it will manifest in the form of shadows. For example, if you repress the higher self, the equivalent of the King or the Queen, depending on whether you are male or female, you will end up behaving as a tyrant or as a weakling. And the link between these two shadows is fear. The tyrant is fearful of being weak, and a weakling is fearful of being tyrannical; that's why they are in these two polarities.

The Great Mother archetype has been repressed for 5,000 years in Western societies—sometimes violently. When an archetype is suppressed that strongly for that long, we begin to consider behavior normal. We forget what the archetype looked like. We forget what a society looked like when a Great Mother archetype was active. So the question becomes: What are the shadows that result from such repression? If we examine our money system, it becomes apparent that greed and fear of scarcity are the shadows our repression has created. Our money system creates an incentive to be greedy and to accumulate through the interest system; and, of course, fear of scarcity is present, because in our society if you don't have money, you'll die.

It's my contention that greed and scarcity are not in nature—not even in human nature. They are built into the money system in which we swim, and we've been swimming in it so long that these shadows have become almost completely transparent to us. We consider it normal and legitimate behavior. It is so legitimate and so normal that when Adam Smith (a Scottish schoolmaster in pre-Victorian times about 200 years ago) studied the system, he concluded that civilized societies are greedy and dealing with scarcity, and he developed a theory called *economics*, which is the allocation of scarce resources through the process of individual greed. The whole process of economics actually has its roots in the two shadows, and the implementation tool—the process by which this becomes real, not just a fictitious concept—is money.

Adam Smith softened the picture by talking about "individual self-satisfaction" rather than greed. Smith suggested that everyone does his own thing for his own selfish purposes, but this kind of behavior can have a positive effect on the whole. Adam Smith's first important book was not the well-known *Wealth of Nations*. It was really *A Treatise on Moral Sentiments* in which he explained in vast detail the different hierarchies of emotions that are legitimate and illegitimate. He didn't really like the concept of greed, but he thought that greed was an important component of any civilized society. You have to understand, of course, that Adam Smith's days were pre-Freud.

That's important to know, because his characterization of economic man is based on an emotionally simplified psychology. Smith posited that economic man was driven by only two emotions: He was desirous of accumulating infinite wealth, and he looked for maximum satisfaction, or utility. There were no motivations other than these two, and these two emotions were the ones that effectively drove the entire economic system.

That economic view is very much a product of our scientific materialism, and it is projected on our material world. It's interesting to note that the words *materialistic* and *matter* come from the

Latin word *mater* (mother)—the words *mother* and *matter* have the same origin. That takes on significance when we realize our belief in materialism is directly related to our repression of the Great Mother archetype. We create a world in which we suppress anything that is not compatible with that reality. We assume, for example, that our economic behavior is universal, but this is not valid, given that we do have booms and crashes. We had them in the 17th century in Holland with tulips, and we have them in real estate in Japan in the early 1990s or in the stock market today. Booms and crashes can't be explained with traditional economic theory.

We have been living in a patriarchal concept of reality for about 5,000 years. I call this the *yang* view of reality. The Chinese terms *yin* and *yang* are quite old, and they describe something very precise; we don't really have an equivalent of these terms in English or other European languages. Yang and yin are necessary complements to each other. They are not polarities. In our language, when I say, "hot," you hear "not cold." In our language, it's built in; we can't think otherwise. In the Chinese concept of yin and yang, however, yang is only yang because of its relationship with yin. Its relationship to yin actually creates it. So what the Chinese look at is the *relationship* between the two. We look at the *difference* between the two. To change our materialistic worldview, we need to look at relationships—the complementary nature of yin and yang.

Most of us probably see the banking system and the economic system as fairly well entrenched. They've been with us for so long. You have some very original views about this, however, based on long years of experience in working with money. How do you think this system is going to be transformed?

First of all, I think the money system is already changing. And the banking system has already changed. The banking system has changed more in 20 years than in the last 300 to 400 years. The function of banks used to be taking deposits from individuals. They pooled the deposits and lent them to businesses. That is what they were doing until the 1970s. Well, because of the information revolution, suddenly everybody can have access to the information for financial market conditions, so corporations decided to borrow directly in the market without going to banks.

They did that by issuing bonds, or commercial paper. They cut the banks out completely. Now that was pretty dramatic. In fact, one-third of the banks in the United States have disappeared since 1980. The banks that did survive managed to do so by switching to credit cards. Credit cards are now the biggest single source of income for many of the largest banks. Credit cards have replaced the loans to businesses. What they used to do for businesses, they now do for individuals through the credit card system.

It's almost as if paper money were becoming an artifact. There's a big emphasis now on electronic banking, where you never see any paper money in the process. Your check goes into your account from your salary, and your bills are paid electronically. It's all automatic.

People talk a lot about electronic commerce. Well, electronic commerce is really just the rest of the economy catching up to where money has been for 30 or 40 years. Electronic reality, virtual space, is the space of money, and it has been that way for at least 20 to 30 years.

You probably have a few bills in your pocket, but that represents only a very small part of the money you have. The rest of the money is probably in a bank account or a brokerage account—which are electronic. That's where 95 percent of our money resides. All our money. Even individual money.

What's important and intriguing—and, depending on your viewpoint, sometimes scary—is that banks are becoming fundamentally communication companies. Conversely, companies that are in communications—telephone companies, computer companies, bill-paying services—are starting to get into banking. Brokers such as Merrill Lynch compete directly with banks. They have CMA accounts, which are basically cash-management accounts that are doing what banks used to do. The process of electronic banking has opened up a whole new reality. In fact, in 5,000 years of the documented history of money, there have been only two major revolutions, and one has happened in our lifetime. The first one was the invention of paper money, which we touched upon earlier, and the second is electronic money. The invention of paper money actually made possible the transfer of the power of issuing money from sovereigns to banks. What electronic money makes possible, we don't know yet. But it is a new game, a totally new game.

Just to give you an idea of what this means, let's look at frequent flyer miles. Frequent flyer miles used to be a little marketing gimmick. Now, you can earn them with all kinds of activities, and you can spend them on all kinds of things. Frequent flyer miles are a medium of exchange—money in the making. They are corporate scrip issued and managed by the airlines. Technically, frequent flyer miles are even taxable. The IRS is usually most innovative in terms of catching where new forms of money come in. Even if you don't use money, you still have to pay taxes on whatever profits you might make on trades by barter, for example.

Cendant, the largest company trading on the Internet, is another example of this. This is a company that nobody's heard of, but it did $1.5 billion in sales in 1997 on the Web, and it offers a million different products and services. A typical K-Mart has 40,000. This company has created its own currency, called Market net cash. And as with frequent flyer miles, with each purchase, you accumulate credit. This, too, is corporate currency in the making. These are two examples of money that already exists, but is not national currency. I predict that the Internet will create other specialized Internet currencies. Why should a German buying a product from an Indian company on the Net have to pay in rupees or in dollars or in Deutsch marks? It doesn't make sense.

There are community currencies as well as Internet currencies in existence. How does that affect the system?

There are 1,400 communities now that have started their own currency system, and it is a very fast-moving field. The number has doubled in only three years. Such systems grow fastest where there is unemployment. There are three main types of local currency. In the United States, you have time-dollars, LETS, and Ithaca hours.

Ithaca hours were started by local activist Paul Glover in Ithaca, New York, about five years ago. It was a unit of account in the hour. If you go to the farmer's market, you see little signs that say "Ithaca Hours Accepted." At the best restaurant in town, you can pay half your bill in Ithaca hours. In the hotel, in the supermarket, you can pay with Ithaca currency. It is a recognized currency. Businesses can accept different percentages of it, depending on how many rounds of them go on expenses and in dollars. A farmer can accept up to 100 percent, since he can keep all the money. It's his own product. On the other hand, the restaurant can only accept 50 percent payment in Ithaca Hours, because it has a good component of cost in dollars that it cannot offset with local currency. But this creates a whole new economic system. Businesses and individuals in the community are basically saying, "In Ithaca We Trust." That's the logo on their currency.

The community is defined, in this case, as a radius of about 50 miles around Ithaca; beyond that, the currency's not acceptable. It's voluntarily kept on a small scale so that the money stays local. It plays the role that a dam would in hydraulics. In other words, it keeps the money where you earned it, where you want it stored and moved around. Otherwise, in many poorer communities, the money just flows out. For example, if you went to the poorest area in Oakland and gave a million dollars out in $100 bills, when you came back 24 hours later to find out where the $100 dollar bills were, you would find that 95 percent of them were no longer in Oakland. They will have been spent on something that immediately went out of the community. In other words, the money flows away from the poorer areas to the richer. Why? Because they have a higher return there.

That reminds me of a story that you wrote about a couple that gave cowrie shells to the bushmen in the Kalahari in the '50s. When the couple went back some time later, they expected to see necklaces of the cowrie shells, but instead they found individual cowrie shells spread all across the Kalahari throughout these bush tribes.

One by one, the shells were given out as a token of appreciation. The bushmen still live in a gift economy. With a gift economy system, things will spread automatically. They will not accumulate.

So the gift economy is where you basically depend on people giving you whatever it is you need to get along. The Buddhist monks, for example, are in a gift economy in Thailand.

Actually, all monks, even Christian monks, participate in a gift economy. One of the rules of the Benedictine Order, for example, prohibits explicit exchanges of money among the members of the community. The reason for that is precisely because you want to create community, and the way of creating community is by gift exchanges. Now what's interesting is that some currencies reinforce community, while others destroy it.

The national currencies, because of the way they are created, basically force competition among participants, while local currencies create cooperation among them. The extreme forms of cooperation are mutual credit systems—things such as time-dollars, where the currency is created by a transaction between two people. When you and I agree on something, for example, you automatically get a credit, and I get a debit of, say, an hour. This would be barter if I did something for you at another time for an hour, but it becomes currency as soon as I start liquidating my debit with someone else in our community, and you can use your credit with someone else again. In other words, it becomes money. Money is created by the transaction itself. That kind of currency, in fact, feeds community.

The word *community* comes from the Latin *communitas*. It literally means "to give among each other." That's why monks or families who want to protect the sense of community do not allow monetary exchanges. Gifts are reciprocal. When I give you something, well, someday, you'll give something back—either to me or to a member of my community. But when you have money exchanges, it's not reciprocal. I give you the money, you give me the item. The deal is over. We don't owe anything to anybody anymore. It's very effective, but it breaks community. What's interesting with the new forms of money we've mentioned—these local currencies—is that they are actually purposely designed money systems that will create community and reinforce it.

Where does the idea of sustainable abundance come into play?

Sustainable abundance may, at first, sound like an oxymoron, a contradiction in terms. Many people think that when something is abundant, it is not sustainable. And it's true in many domains. If I try to sustain an abundance of timber, I'm not going to have many forests left. I'm going to cut all the trees down. If I have an abundance of cars, I'm going to have a lot of pollution and traffic jams. So there are domains where it is a contradiction. On the other hand, there are other domains where that's not the case. If we concentrate on the specific areas where sustainable abundance is not contradictory, we can actually solve many of the problems that we are facing today. An obvious case is knowledge. We are moving into an information and knowledge society. Information and knowledge become much cheaper to access than ever before. We have an extraordinary opportunity to actually make information available on a global level—at an extraordinarily cheap price. The more people know, the more sustainable they become.

Another domain that could assist sustainable abundance is money itself. The national currency system is based on scarcity; the currency has to remain scarce in order to remain valuable. That is the way it's designed. Scarcity doesn't really lie in the world; it lies in the money.

We could have two kinds of currency systems that are complementary to each other. Today, we only have one that we emphasize, and we consider it the only one that is valid—and that is the national dollar currency. There is no reason that it should remain the only one, and as we mentioned, other systems are already developing. There are thousands of communities that have done this. It can be done. It *is* being done. And it has extraordinary results. People can create real wealth for themselves as a community. By combining national currency with local currencies, you can actually solve many of the problems that we now face. Just make a list of all the good ideas you know about that have not materialized because of a lack of money. If you are living in a community, you can agree to use something other than national currencies for your exchanges, and you suddenly solve the scarcity factor. So that is one of the keys.

Curitiba, a city in southern Brazil, is a good example of this. It's about 400 kilometers south of São Paulo. Here is a city that has a standard of living far above the rest of Brazil. It is the first city in Latin America to move out of the Third World in one generation.

About a third of the income of a typical Curitiban is not in the national currency. It is in goods and services provided by a parallel system. One component of the parallel system happens to be garbage. The Curitibans change garbage into money. This is an innovative approach to their situation. In Brazil, there are many poor areas, without streets, so there is no way of bringing in garbage trucks. The traditional solution would be to throw some money at it, destroy everything, build the roads, and solve the problem.

About 15 years ago, the mayor of Curitiba did something different. He said, "For any bag of sorted garbage, we'll give you a token. And the token gives you value for a trip on the bus system." This is one of the most advanced bus systems in the world. It was used by *Scientific American* as an example for town organization in terms of public transportation. So, these tokens became currency—and garbage became money.

The mayor created a whole parallel economy using tokens, and the tokens are not scarce. If you have another bag of garbage, he can give you another token. He doesn't have to go to the central bank in Brasilia to ask for them. He creates these things himself. The results are quite impressive. Curitiba has received an award from the United Nations for being the most ecological city in the world. They have 55 square meters per inhabitant of green area, accessible to the public in the city. They have Bach chorales; they have music festivals. They have a free university—all because they have been able to use two parallel economic systems to their advantage.

What's the first step to creating this kind of community?

First, gather your community and start talking about what you want to do and how you want to do it. There are websites available for choosing the kind of money system that would be most conducive for what you are trying to do. It depends on the scale. It depends on the technology you are going to use. There are a variety of options already available. The main point is if you have agreement, you can create a currency and address your problems locally. By having a currency, you can take your future in your own hands.

⁂

EPILOGUE

Bernard Lietaer presents a vision of the future of money, which challenges conventional wisdom and traditional financial structures. He maintains that changes in how we relate to money are inevitable, because the wheels of transformation are grinding globally and will organically catalyze much of the change.

Mostly, his contribution forces us to ask new questions and to consider fresh scenarios and possibilities. Meaningful work, rebuilding community, and a sustainable world are all part of rethinking the money system, and he points out that this is not theory, but rather is based on pragmatic examples emerging all over the planet. In the end, it is a hopeful vision and one that can help sustain us as we recreate our relationship to money in the 21st century.

❋ ❋ ❋ ❋ ❋ ❋

Appendix

RECOMMENDED READING

The Abundance Book, by John Randolph Price

Best 75 Business Practices for Socially Responsible Companies, by Alan Reder

Creating True Prosperity, by Shakti Gawain

Creative Visualization, by Shakti Gawain

Investing from the Heart: The Guide to Socially Responsible Investments, by Alan Reder and Jack A. Brill

The Little Money Bible, by Stuart Wilde

Money and the Meaning of Life, by Jacob Needleman

The Prosperity Handbook, by C. Holland Taylor

In Pursuit of Principle and Profit, by Alan Reder

Real Wealth: A Spiritual Approach to Money and Work, by Jonathan Robinson

The Soul of Business, with Michael Toms, Charles Garfield, and Other Contributors

Time and the Soul: Where Has All the Meaningful Time Gone? by Jacob Needleman

True Wealth: An Innovative Guide to Dealing with Money in Our Lives, by Paul Hwoschinsky

True Work: The Sacred Dimension of Earning a Living, by Justine Willis Toms and Michael Toms

The Well of Creativity, with Michael Toms, Julia Cameron, and Other Contributors

Your Money or Your Life: Transforming Your Relationship with Money and Achieving Financial Independence, by Joe Dominguez and Vicki Robin

New Dimensions Audiocassettes

These audiocassettes are the word-for-word recordings of the original radio conversations from which *Money, Money, Money* was compiled.

MONEYPOWER AND PROSPERITY PRINCIPLES, with **C. HOLLAND TAYLOR**. Beyond the usual jargon and political doublespeak surrounding economic concerns, Taylor addresses the issue of money directly and clearly. Honesty at all levels, voluntary cooperation, and seeing through the ways money is manipulated by the "system" hold the key to greater personal economic understanding. Dedication, persistence, and the ability to accept and grow with change are crucial if personal economic problems are to be solved, according to Taylor. As people learn to navigate the money maze, economic problems will be solved individually and collectively. Taylor is the co-author of *The Prosperity Handbook* (Communications Research, 1984).

Tape #1896 1 hr. $9.95

MONEYWISE, with **JOE DOMINGUEZ**. It is possible to attain mastery of money and become financially independent, according to Dominguez, who himself has been financially independent since 1969 and takes no money for anything he does. Simple, yet profound, his message goes to the core of how money works and provides pragmatic insights about handling money. He goes far beyond the usual financial advice to address deeper issues such as how money is connected to life energy and the source of our views about money. For anyone wanting to create financial clarity, Dominguez provides a new road map. He is the creator of the seminar-on-tape, "Transforming Your Relationship with Money and Achieving Financial Independence."

Tape #2119 1 hr. $9.95

WHERE RICHES LIE, with **PAUL HWOSCHINSKY**. Money and wealth are not the same thing, asserts Hwoschinsky, a venture capitalist, wilderness photographer, and author of *True Wealth* (Ten-Speed Press, 1990). By using a "nonfinancial balance sheet" to identify the assets which, more than money ever could, indicate our aliveness and true wealth—our health, relationships, education, vision, and creativity—we can begin to integrate them with our financial assets to connect who we really are with what we do. "Must" listening for rich, poor and in-between.

Tape #2229 1 hr. $9.95

MONEY AND SPIRIT, with **JACOB NEEDLEMAN**. "Money has become for our generation what sex was for the earlier generations," says philosopher Jacob Needleman, "a force that is at the back of almost everything people do, but which we're not yet able to face without hypocrisy." In this refreshingly candid and insightful interview, Needleman discusses the meaning of money and its place in the spiritual life, and how we can all learn from our own attitudes toward it. He is the author of *The Heart of Philosophy* (Bantam, 1984) and *Money and the Meaning of Life* (Doubleday, 1991).

Tape #2241 1 hr. $9.95

MONEY SENSE, with **JOE DOMINGUEZ** and **VICKI ROBIN**. Have you mastered money in your life, or does it master you? Dominguez and Robin describe their own philosophy and techniques for knowing "how much is enough," for living below your means and not needing to work for money. They challenge us in new ways to reexamine our relationship to money and things financial. Dominguez is the author of the "Transforming Your Relationship with Money and Achieving Financial Independence" audiocassette/workbook course, distributed by the New Road Map Foundation, of which Vicki Robin is president, which also raises significant financial support for a variety of nonprofit organizations.

Tape #2246 1 hr. $9.95

MONEY FOR GOOD, with **ALAN REDER**. We all know that money talks. Now learn how to make it speak for your values and beliefs, no matter how much or how little you have to invest. You can put your money to work to support your ethical beliefs, allowing you to feel great about the world your money is helping to build—and you don't have to sacrifice a penny of investment profit to keep your ethic intact. In this interview, Reder explores the rapidly expanding movement of socially responsible investing. Reder says, "Create a better world—invest in it." He is the co-author, with Jack A. Brill, of *Investing from the Heart: The Guide to Socially Responsible Investments and Money Management* (Crown Publishers, 1992).

Tape #2323 1 hr. $9.95

THE SOUL OF MONEY, with **LYNNE TWIST**. Want an eye-opening experience? Pick up your checkbook—and read it. For better or worse, it is a self-portrait of who you are and the choices you have been making about your priorities in life. Now listen to this luminous and inspiring vision of how to make money a true partner in expressing and fulfilling your highest beliefs and values. This is one of the most powerful and exciting voices we have heard lately, reminding us of what's really important in life. "In our society," Twist says, "money is the voice of your commitment....Let's use money—the thing that people think is so evil—to bring in the light, to transform the future." She is a global fund-raiser *par excellence*, and a founding executive of the Hunger Project, dedicated to ending chronic hunger worldwide. Hear "how to use money as another avenue to express the soulful human being that we are."

Tape #2595 1 hr. $9.95

TRUE PROSPERITY, with **SHAKTI GAWAIN**. When most of us think of prosperity, we immediately think of money. Shakti Gawain has another definition: "Prosperity is the experience of having what we truly need and want in life. Prosperity is an experience; it doesn't come from anything external." Without disregarding the important role money plays, Gawain believes that problems with money often point toward some spiritual or emotional block or area of needed healing. Recognizing that we are here, after all, to do more than make lots of money frees us to pursue our deepest longings and discard false desires that serve neither heart nor soul. Shakti Gawain is a workshop leader and pioneer in the fields of creativity, intuition, and expanding consciousness and is a publisher and author of ten books, including the best-selling classic *Creative Visualization* (New World Library, revised 1995). Her latest book is *Creating True Prosperity* (New World Library, 1997).

Tape #2696 1 hr. $9.95

THE FUTURE OF MONEY, with **BERNARD LIETAER**. Where does money come from? What is it, really? And how can we use it in a way that strengthens and enriches life in our local communities? Bernard Lietaer, a visionary with a long background in banking and economics, offers incisive and seldom-heard ideas about the history and future of money, the impact of electronic banking and the Internet, and how alternative currencies are being used to actually create wealth in small communities. This dialogue is an eye-opening excursion through the mysteries of money, and presents a new way of looking at economics and new possibilities for building community and economic well-being. "The good news here," says Lietaer, "is that people can choose their currency. You could do this yourself. You don't need permission from anybody." Formerly with the National Bank of Belgium, Lietaer is a research fellow at the Center for Sustainable Resources at the University of California, Berkeley, and visiting psychology professor at Sonoma State University.

Tape #2702 1 Hour $9.95

TO ORDER TAPES

Call toll free: (800) 935-8273. Each tape is $9.95 unless otherwise noted, plus postage, shipping, and handling.

Books, Audios, and More from New Dimensions Foundation

(available through Hay House)

Books

Buddhism in the West—The Dalai Lama and other contributors
Money, Money, Money—Jacob Needleman and other contributors
The Power of Meditation and Prayer—Larry Dossey, M.D., and other contributors
Roots of Healing—Andrew Weil, M.D., and other contributors
The Soul of Business—Charles Garfield and other contributors
The Well of Creativity—Julia Cameron and other contributors

Audios

(All of the audios below feature New Dimensions Radio co-founder Michael Toms interviewing some of the foremost thinkers and social innovators of our time.)

The Art of Soul Work—Thomas Moore
Authentic Power—Gary Zukav
Future Medicine—Daniel Goleman
Healing from the Inside Out—Bernie Siegel, M.D.
Healing with Spirit—Caroline Myss, Ph.D.
The Heart of Spiritual Practice—Jack Kornfield
Live Long and Feel Good—Andrew Weil, M.D.
Make Your Dreams Real—Barbara Sher
Making Magic in the World—Maya Angelou
Medicine, Meaning, and Prayer—Larry Dossey, M.D.
Messages of the Celestine Prophecy—James and Salle Redfield
A New Approach to Medicine—Andrew Weil, M.D.
The New Millennium—Jean Houston, Ph.D.
Psychic and Intuitive Healing—Barbara Brennan, Rosalyn Bruyere, and Judith Orloff, M.D.
Roots of Healing—Andrew Weil, M.D., and others
Sacred Odyssey—Ram Dass
True Work—Justine Willis Toms and Michael Toms (audio book)
The Wisdom of Joseph Campbell—Joseph Campbell

Calendar

Wise Words: Perennial Wisdom from the New Dimensions Radio Series

(To order the products above, please call Hay House at 800-654-5126.)

New Dimensions Foundation

Since its inception in 1973, New Dimensions Foundation has presented lecture series, live events, and seminars; published books, sponsored educational tours, and launched a major periodical. Created to address the dramatic cultural shifts and changing human values in our society, New Dimensions has become an international forum for some of the most innovative ideas expressed on the planet. Its principal and best-known activity is New Dimensions Radio, an independent producer of radio dialogues and other programming.

During the past 25 years, many of this century's leading thinkers and social innovators have spoken through New Dimensions. The programming supports a diversity of views from many traditions and cultures. Now is a time for transformative learning and for staying open to all possibilities. We must constantly be willing to review and revise what we are creating. New Dimensions fosters the goals of living a more healthy life of mind, body, and spirit while deepening our connections to self, family, community, environment, and planet.

New Dimensions is a rare entity in the world of media—a completely independent, noncommercial radio producer. Primary support comes from listeners. Members of "Friends of New Dimensions" (FOND) are active partners in a community of hope as we celebrate the human spirit and explore new ideas, provocative insights, and creative solutions across the globe over the airwaves.

You too can play an invaluable part in this positive force for change by becoming a member of FOND and supporting the continued production and international distribution of New Dimensions Radio programming.

Become a Member of FOND

As a Member of "Friends of New Dimensions" (FOND), you will receive:

- The *New Dimensions Journal,* a bimonthly magazine containing captivating articles, reviews of books, video and audio tapes, current "New Dimensions" program schedules, selections of audio tapes from our archives, and much more.
- The New Dimensions Annual Tape Catalog and periodic supplements.
- A 15% discount on any product purchased through New Dimensions, including books, New Dimensions tapes, and selected tapes from other producers.
- A quality thank-you gift expressing our deepest appreciation.
- The satisfaction of knowing that you are supporting the broadcast of hopeful visions to people all across the nation and the world.

Contributions are tax deductible to the extent allowed by law.
With Visa, Mastercard, or Discover, please call (800) 935-8273.

⁂ NOTES ⁂

❋ Notes ❋

❋ NOTES ❋

⁂ NOTES ⁂

❋ NOTES ❋

❋ ❋ ❋

We hope you enjoyed
this Hay House/New Dimensions book.
If you would like to receive a free catalog featuring additional
Hay House books and products, or if you would like
information about the Hay Foundation,
please contact:

Hay House, Inc.
P.O. Box 5100
Carlsbad, CA 92018-5100

(760) 431-7695 or (800) 654-5126
(760) 431-6948 (fax) or (800) 650-5115 (fax)

Please visit the Hay House Website at:
www.hayhouse.com
and the New Dimensions Website at:
www.newdimensions.org

❋ ❋ ❋